"The issue of refugees and immigrants exposes the division in America today. It also brings to light how many Christians see the issues more as a political football than as being about people for whom Jesus died. In *No Longer Strangers*, a remarkable group of contributors with deep and diverse experience in ministry to the marginalized show how to be incarnational in our evangelism. God is bringing the nations to us; may we be faithful to Jesus as we seek justice, show mercy, and tell the good news."

— ED STETZER

dean of the School of Mission, Ministry,
and Leadership at Wheaton College

"*No Longer Strangers* makes a significant and insightful contribution to the ongoing discussion about Christianity and immigration. The authors understand that each person who wishes to immigrate is created in the image and likeness of God and should be treated as such, including in how the gospel is brought to them. This book provides a vision of what that looks like for the church. It is not the first word or the last word on the topic, but it is an important word for all church leaders and Christians doing evangelism with immigrant communities. The authors raise good questions. As you wrestle with both the problems and the proposed solutions, you will be inspired to think about ministry in your context. You'll be grateful you read this book—you'll be more self-aware as a Christian and better able to equip your church for Christlike engagement with your immigrant neighbors."

— J. D. GREEAR

pastor of The Summit Church and 62nd president of
the Southern Baptist Convention

"We have forgotten as an American church what it means to engage in a healthy, holistic, and effective evangelism. We have been operating a sports car with eight cylinders on only two cylinders. Eugene Cho and Samira Izadi Page have edited an important volume that engages the significance of evangelism while recognizing the power of the gospel at work in the marginalized communities. This book calls us to rediscover an expression of biblical Christian faith that does not ignore those who will form the spiritual backbone of the next evangelicalism."

— SOONG-CHAN RAH
author of *The Next Evangelicalism:*
Freeing the Church from Western Cultural Captivity

"God is up to something dramatic. The mass migration that now brings us into contact with people from every tribe, tongue, and nation is both a profound privilege and a daunting responsibility. This book is a deeply important and much-needed guide to how we can live out the gospel in its fullness to the treasured 'strangers among us.' It will inspire and challenge in equal measure—and will stir your spiritual imagination to new expressions of a worthy witness."

— SCOTT ARBEITER
president of World Relief

NO LONGER STRANGERS

*Transforming Evangelism with
Immigrant Communities*

Edited by

EUGENE CHO AND SAMIRA IZADI PAGE

William B. Eerdmans Publishing Company
Grand Rapids, Michigan

Wm. B. Eerdmans Publishing Co.
4035 Park East Court SE, Grand Rapids, Michigan 49546
www.eerdmans.com

27 26 25 24 23 22 21   1 2 3 4 5 6 7

ISBN 978-0-8028-7865-6

Library of Congress Cataloging-in-Publication Data

Names: Cho, Eugene, editor. | Page, Samira Izadi, editor.
Title: No longer strangers : transforming evangelism with immigrant communities / edited by Eugene Cho and Samira Izadi Page.
Description: Grand Rapids, Michigan : William B. Eerdmans Publishing Company, 2021. | Includes bibliographical references and index. | Summary: "A multi-perspective guide to doing the work of evangelism with immigrants and refugees in a way that is sensitive to the dynamics of differences in culture, race, and language"—Provided by publisher.
Identifiers: LCCN 2020045491 | ISBN 9780802878656 (paperback)
Subjects: LCSH: Church work with immigrants. | Church work with refugees. | Evangelistic work.
Classification: LCC BV639.I4 N6 2021 | DDC 269/.2086912—dc23
LC record available at https://lccn.loc.gov/2020045491

For everyone the gospel brings together—
may we no longer be strangers

CONTENTS

CONTENTS

FOREWORD

Just on the edge of Jesus's hometown of Capernaum stands a statue, and no one would be surprised if you miss it—I nearly walked right by it.

Because the statue isn't of a lofty, neoclassical crowned figure, isn't of a robed goddess with arm stretched out as a beacon of light, isn't a patinated icon of particular optimism.

The statue is of a homeless figure sleeping on a park bench. Face and hands shrouded under a blanket pulled around him tight, the figure seems nameless—until you see his bare and uncovered feet that the blanket can't reach.

The exposed feet of the homeless guy bear nail wounds.

The nameless man is the roofless Jesus.

I wanted to touch his feet.

I wanted to reach out and cover his feet, somehow offer the God-man some kind of shelter. To somehow warm the sojourner who pulled a thin cover up over himself with the cold reality that "Foxes have holes, and birds of the air have nests, but the Son of Man has nowhere to lay his head."

The life of Jesus is the life of a wanderer.

I stood there, struck that the statue to honor the God of the universe right outside his hometown depicts a man who had no home. The guy who came to grant us liberty—and welcome us home—was in reality wandering without a home.

If Jesus qualified as homeless, is there something shamefully disqualifying about needing a home and the help of community?

Do those who believe in his all-sufficient grace support welcoming only those who are self-sufficient—and not those in desperate need?

We are all the same in that every single one of us is different—and that doesn't affect our value any differently. Where you're from should never determine how anyone's going to treat you.

Regardless of citizenship, everyone, by God, has earned the dignity of personhood.

~~~

I once stood at the Mexican border wall and reached my hand through to pray with a woman on the other side. She still had scissors in her hand.

She'd been bent down, rummaging through garbage heaps, just on the other side of the wall, plucking out plastic bottles, to cut the tops off for manipulatives in her kids' classrooms. But she'd come near, and here we were praying, me holding her hand through a slot in the border wall while she was standing there holding a pair of scissors.

It looked like we were about to cut through all the noise to hear the heart of God—much like the book in your hand is about to cut through the confusion of these times so that you can hear the beat of God's heart.

Through the slats in the wall, just past her, just behind her, was a steeple topped with a cross. When I looked over at her—I could see the cruciform symbol of the church everywhere—I could see light in the woman's kind eyes. The only way to see Jesus is to look at the person across from you and see that person through the cross.

The person on the other side of things is always an image of Jesus. Christ is the one in every crisis. And Christ is in the crisis at all the borders—and often the crisis is at the borders, too, of our comfortableness, at the edges of our faithfulness. The voices that speak in this book will help navigate those borders within and the borders around us and guide us toward deeper faithfulness.

There at the wall, back behind me was a cross atop a mountain. It faced her, and that, coupled with the cross atop the church on the other side of the wall, which faced me, made me wonder whether, when we make someone else into "the other," we have made for ourselves a god other than the One who died on the cross.

She said she had seven children. I told her I did too. And she pointed at me, eyebrows raised—you too? I grinned and tried to joke how we were both mothers of one and a half-dozen kids, and she and I, we laughed loudly in the wind, because true, good news lets everything that destroys empathy blow away like hot air and laughs with hope of healing at the days to come. We are all more alike than we like to think we're all different.

We find ourselves in days where it's too often considered a radical, dangerous act to simply see our shared humanity. But in actual fact, maybe it's far more dangerous when we can't see that. What if we leaned in and listened to voices and stories and sat with the hope that we are family not because we have the same nationality—but because we bear the image of the same God. What if we were a society that wasn't so profoundly image conscious but was more profoundly conscious of the image of God in each other? What if we were less devoted to projecting a certain image and were more devoted to protecting the image of God in each other?

What if we took time to honestly ask ourselves: Why in the world are we all born where we are born?

Where we live has to mean more than getting something—it has to mean that to those who have been given much, much will be required.

It has to mean that those who have privilege can't live indifferently but are meant to live differently so others can simply live.

It has to mean that we are living meaningful lives only if we are help-ing others get to live meaningful lives.

Those seeking a meaningful life no matter where they have to go are seeking exactly what we are. They aren't like "animals or criminals"—they are like us.

And yes, it's true, the world and governments are complicated, but what isn't complicated is that outreach can change the world like outrage never will. What isn't complicated is that every single believer has to wrestle with the fact that God's commandment to care for the stranger is

more important to God than the other commandments in the Torah—
even more important than the commandment to love God.

Does God command us to love the stranger more than he commands us to love himself because loving the stranger is how we love
God himself?

Does the Torah instruct care for the stranger far more than it commands rest on the Sabbath or any other law because God doesn't want
us to rest until all laws find ways to care for the stranger?

I looked into the eyes of the mama of seven just like me, just on the
other side of the line, who is living in a world of people who want just
what we all want—a good life for our families.

~~~

The crisis at the borders of the world isn't about violent criminals; it is
about those genuinely seeking asylum from violence and criminals.

Seeking asylum isn't a dangerously wrong thing to do; it's a human
thing to do when you're in danger.

This conversation about immigration isn't about disregarding the law
but about how to regard people made in the image of God.

And this conversation isn't about open borders; it is about being
open to the compassionate, humane treatment of fellow human beings
who are trying to make the best decisions for their families, just as we
are trying to do for our families. So, how do we treat them as we would
want to be treated?

Abraham, one of the fathers of faith, told a lie at the Egyptian border,
and told his wife to lie, because he was driven by starvation and desperation.
How can we have anything but compassion for the same motivation?

Those who find themselves behind bars are not always against God
or good laws: Samson, Joseph, Stephen, Jeremiah, Peter, Shadrach, Meshach, Abednego, Silas, John the Baptist, Paul, and Jesus himself, the perfecter of our faith, were all jailed for seemingly breaking a law, but man's
laws are not always God's laws, and laws change all the time, and laws can
change to reflect how our hearts are reflecting more of God's laws.

The faithful always believe there are ways to shape laws to be faithfully just and faithfully compassionate.

The faithful believe there are ways to have a deeply robust pro-life ethic, and be pro-pro-pro:

- pro-life, which is to be pro-life for all life, including a refugee's life
- pro-security, which is to be pro-life for all life, including every community's life
- pro-flourishing, which is to be pro-life for all life, including the economic flourishing of every community.

Believers have to believe there are nuanced, considered ways to not create an "either/or" world but a "pro-pro-pro" world.

Christians need not all agree on laws around immigration, but we all need to find real ways to move into Jesus's kind heart toward those in need.

~~~

The woman on the other side of the wall, she patted my hand gently and I nodded: If any national citizenship is prioritized more than our citizenship in heaven and the care of all the citizens of earth, can any of us claim discipleship of Jesus?

In that church right behind the woman whose hand I was holding, I knew what they read—because it's the same thing read in evangelical churches around the world: how Jesus is not only compassionate to individual persons in need but is also passionate about the structural policies that prevent showing compassion to persons in need (Luke 6:6–11). We are truly caring about people only when we care about the policies that are truly affecting people.

And I wanted to somehow find words and tell the woman on the other side of the wall how I wonder which side of the fence I'm actually standing on.

Do I stand on the side Jesus calls the Blessed: blessed are the poor, blessed are those who mourn, blessed are those who hunger and seek for rightness . . . for they are on the right side of history?

Or do I stand on the side Jesus calls out with the Anti-Beatitudes of the Multitudes—the Four Woes of the Comfortable:

> "But woe to you who are rich,
>> for you have already received your comfort.
> Woe to you who are well fed now,
>> for you will go hungry.
> Woe to you who laugh now,
>> for you will mourn and weep.
> Woe to you when everyone speaks well of you,
>> for that is how their ancestors treated the false
>> prophets"? (Luke 6:24–26 NIV)

Woe to those who are rich in comfort now, who are well fed now, who laugh now, who are spoken well of now . . . for they are on the wrong side of things for all eternity.

I looked down at my feet on this side—and her feet on the other side.

Maybe those of us who are on the comfortable side of things now will be on the hellish side of things forever.

And those who are on the poor side of things now will be on the blessed side of things forever.

Which side of things you are on now decides which side of forever you are on.

~~~

I looked up and looked her in the eye. As a Canadian family, we personally sponsored other families to come live in our community, first a Middle Eastern family of six from the war-torn apocalypse that is Aleppo, Syria, and then an African family of five from the tangled bloodshed that has been the Congo. But in that moment all I could see was Jesus:

Share what you have now, or you'll have your share of woe forever.

My chest was burning with conviction, and I tightened my grip on my sister's hand on the other side of the wall, and I could hear it loud, reverberating off all the walls within, and it was like the rocks and the ground and the crosses on both sides of the wall were crying out with the Word of God and it was all I could hear, standing there:

"For he himself is our peace, who has made the two groups one and has destroyed the barrier, the dividing wall of hostility" (Eph. 2:14 NIV).

A moment can speak to you, cut right to the quick—if you let it.

~~~

I once stood in Iraq with a man who looked me straight in the eye and said: "The world doesn't see me as human," and he turned and leaned in so I could see the screaming whites of his eyes, so I could feel the begging warm breath of his heart when he whispered, "Even dogs can flee danger, and you? You can wing your way back to your island of safety—but I'm stuck here in the middle of all this warring to breathe as a nonhuman, and there is no one—no united nations, no united peoples, no united front—no one who cares how I exist, where I exist, or if I exist."

~~~

I once held a refugee from the Congo who had witnessed the blade of a machete splaying open the veins of her mother's neck, and she turned and ran, for weeks she ran, barefoot across whole countries, and her tears ran down over the torture that scars her cheeks, ran salty down my arm, her words running right into me: "Why was my life supposed to be like this?"

~~~

I once knelt with a woman who was raped thousands of times in Syria, body and soul bought, owned, and traded for years, by men masked in black, and she howled to the heavens when they slammed her baby boy's head up against the cement walls like a rat to be smashed.

And when I reached out to tenderly touch her son's now twisted ear, I wondered if the world heard over the roar of violence, over the fleeing of running feet, the cries that just plead:

Please.

Please.

Dignity and humanity are not a function of geography or nationality. And worth is not based on where you breathe in this world.

When you did not choose for your roof to be the open, devouring mouth of ravenous violence, where in the world can you, and your wide-eyed children, find anyone who will just choose to say:

Welcome?

~~~

A couple hundred feet away from the center of Jesus's hometown of Capernaum, St. Peter's Church rises above an archaeological dig that discovered a first-century church—what is now regarded as the "first church in the world."

And just beyond that first church in the world, you can hear the waves of the Sea of Galilee lapping endlessly, begging to be heard right there at the feet of the Christ who was a refugee, who was a migrant.

If some statues stand as a symbol for an idea of welcome and liberty and freedom to come and know hope, maybe in Jesus's hometown this statue of the Homeless Jesus lying down on a park bench is about the laying down of our lives to embrace the idea of welcoming in.

Maybe the Father of Exiles, the Exiled Man himself, is asking us to see his presence among the exiles, to wake and see his face among the desperate wanderers of the world, to hear the aching cry of "Why is there no safe place for me?"

To grow deaf and blind to the plight of the afflicted is to commit the gravest injustice.

To rise to aid the downtrodden has always been the choice of the greatest.

Making one's own interests always first is a way to end up eternally last.

I had knelt down right there by the homeless depiction of Christ with his bare and scarred feet exposed to the elements. I'd looked across to the world's very first church that stands on the teeming shore of Jesus's hometown.

What if Jesus comes in the disguise of the desperate immigrant or refugee, and to refuse him is to refuse one's identity as an evangelical who welcomes others into good news?

What if people of good news could still hear the heartbeat of the homeless God-man under the sheet, and be the welcome of his church?

> "Give me your tired who can't find a place to lay their head,
>   your direly poor who are struggling to stand on their
>   two feet,
>   so they can know the love of those who are the hands
>   and feet
>   of Jesus, who never refuses those treated like refuse.
>
> "Give me those who believe
>   there is a beacon of possibility that still blazes bright
>   only because
>   it's hospitably open to the oxygen of opportunity
>   beyond itself,
>   only because it believes that if it shutters itself closed under
>   a basket,
>   it will wane away in the dark.
>
> "Send me those seeking a roof for their wounds,
>   courage for their crises, hope for their hunger.
>   Send these, the homeless, trauma-tossed to me,
>   because I am the rising Light, I am the open door!"

Before I could bring myself to leave the wandering Jesus, before reluctantly walking out of Jesus's hometown carrying with me Jesus's mandate of liberty and hospitality, something in me opened wider, something like a biblical charge for everyone who knows how the good news can heal the hurting, a charge that I couldn't blithely ignore:

"As you did it to one of the least of my brothers and sisters, you did it to me."

—Ann Voskamp
author of the *New York Times* best sellers
The Broken Way and *One Thousand Gifts*

ACKNOWLEDGMENTS

No book is ever written in isolation because humans simply don't live in isolation. In that spirit, we want to acknowledge and thank the many individuals and partners who contributed to the writing of this resource . . . for the purpose of challenging and encouraging the church.

Foremost, thanks to the many refugees and immigrants from all over the country who shared their lives and stories with us. Sharing one's story in itself takes courage and vulnerability, and we are humbled that they've trusted us to steward their stories.

We'd like to thank Dr. Elaine Heath, former dean of Duke Divinity School, for believing in this project, connecting leaders to the original group of collaborators, and giving the project its initial support. We'd also like to thank Dr. Edgardo Colón-Emeric of Duke Divinity School and the director of the Center for Reconciliation, as well as Abi Riak—then director of operations for the center—for their thoughtful contribution to the tone and direction of the work. We are grateful to the Center for Reconciliation for investing in and hosting the initial group meetings between authors and editors.

Many thanks to various voices from different parts of World Relief, such as Zach Bond, Damon Schroeder, Jenn Yang, Gil Odendaal, Matt Soerens, and others who contributed their networks, time, prayer, and insights to help form the vision for this book from the beginning. Zach, you helped get this whole thing started.

Thanks to Eerdmans Publishing and their fantastic team for investing in this resource for Christians everywhere who are navigating how to relate to and love their immigrant neighbors as themselves.

Of course, we want to extend deep gratitude to all our authors and storytellers for their wisdom, patience, and love for the church, which is so evident in the care they took in treading sensitively and truthfully in a place of pain and promise for the church.

We want particularly to thank Adam Clark, who not only served as the project manager for this book during his spare time but also, in his full time, embodies the very spirit and convictions of this book through his leadership as director of World Relief Durham. While his name may not be listed in the table of contents or on its cover, this book would not have been possible without him.

And lastly, thanks to Jesus Christ, our light, our leader, the great healer of harms and the pioneer who is showing all of us a better way to live in light of God's love. During these challenging and disruptive times, may we in the church continue to fix our eyes upon Jesus, the author and perfecter of our faith. To God be the glory and honor. Amen.

INTRODUCTION

We believe that this book is both very timely and utterly important—particularly for the North American and Western church. As most know, the topic of immigrants and refugees is all over the airwaves and even emanates from pulpits these days. While this work is incredibly complex, nuanced, and challenging, we are encouraged that more and more Christians and churches are seeking to respond, including through evangelism. The editors of this volume and the contributors believe wholeheartedly that evangelism is a necessary and beautiful part of our discipleship. However, while the book affirms the important commitment of evangelism, we highlight the dangers when North American Christians, in particular, underestimate how their education, race, language mastery, and other factors impact their ability to love and express the gospel (in word and deed) to refugees and immigrants coming from backgrounds that include trauma, oppression, colonialism, persecution, etc.

Our commitment to this book is to balance the prophetic, pastoral, practical, and personal. It's with this objective in mind that we've prayerfully assembled renowned and respected pastors, practitioners, and theologians to help create this resource for individuals, churches, nonprofits, mission organizations, and theological institutions. Additionally, we've gathered firsthand testimonies of immigrants and refugees themselves because we believe it is important to elevate, hear, and learn from their voices.

Our aim is for this book to provide the necessary tools for churches, individuals, and leaders to be more informed about current cultural, social, and economic dynamics involved in working with refugees, immigrants, and the displaced. Understanding these dynamics will provide a framework for effective, healthy, and restorative discipleship and evangelism as it relates to gospel witness. Stories, experiences, anecdotes, and Scripture presented from multiple perspectives (and authors) will help address:

- misconceptions and assumptions: about discipleship, evangelism, immigrants, refugees, and those who are displaced
- tension of the past: historical ways in which evangelism and discipleship have been harmful
- current dynamics: trauma, oppression, grief, ethnocentrism
- reimagining the future: alternative scriptural paradigms for discipleship and evangelism that are restorative

Serving the vulnerable and the displaced is considered an integral part of Christian mission, as is preaching the gospel of Jesus Christ in the terms of the Great Commission. However, due to the growing complexities of power, race, class, and religion, churches need postcolonial guidance and direction to understand what healthy evangelism looks like: evangelism that does not hurt but heals. This book, through the sharing of experiences, expertise, and diverse lenses, will guide churches, individuals, and Christian leaders in the ways of healthy discipleship and instruct them in how to avoid evangelism that causes harm to immigrants through abuses of power dynamics and intercultural blind spots. Healthy evangelism will be defined in scriptural terms in relation to the cultural, social, and economic dynamics at play for immigrants and refugees.

Right discipleship begins with a proper understanding of the Great Commission. The church and Christians who make up her body must act on her behalf to care for the vulnerable, the refugee, and the immigrant. Throughout history, the Christian church has employed discipleship in the form of evangelism that has hurt more than it has helped. Christians of today need to use more informed ways to help current refugees and immigrants. Understanding the psychological impact of trauma, oppression, and grief that immigrants and refugees are often facing should change the way the church disciples and witnesses to the vulnerable. Instead of an ethnocentric paradigm, a new paradigm is presented that is faithful to the Great Commission and is also restorative in nature. Ultimately, readers of this book will be equipped with the necessary skills to not only speak about discipleship to immigrants in a healthy way but also live it out in a dynamic and evangelistic way—a way that recognizes and treats immigrants as equal partners in the mission of God.

When a group of us were asked to participate in this book project, we prayed, sought guidance from the Holy Spirit, brainstormed, and came up with different areas that needed to be considered as well as additional persons to speak to the discussion on how evangelism has brought both pain and healing to immigrants. It is humbling to know that God has entrusted us and has seen fit for the church to serve the most vulnerable populations, namely, refugees and immigrants. We considered our call as Christians to serve people who have been uprooted and abused, people whose dignity has been stolen from them, often by their own people and governments, in the name of God and religion. "The thief comes only to steal and kill and destroy. I came that they may have life, and have it abundantly," Jesus says (John 10:10).[1] How do we share the good news of the abundant life in Christ with disenfranchised and wounded people? How do we share God's love with people who are disillusioned by religion and have little or no trust in anyone who wants to push yet another religious agenda into their already broken lives?

Why should we write on evangelism with a focus on refugees and immigrants at this particular time? Some may have strong opinions about the issue of refugees and immigrants, depending on where they fall on the political spectrum. The issue of evangelizing immigrants, refugees, and other marginalized groups in society can feel like a new problem, and oftentimes can seem political and intimidating or even scary to us. We live in a strange and fast-changing world. Our communities and society are rapidly changing. Some of us may feel like our way of life is being invaded by people who don't know and appreciate our system and values. At no point in history has the world ever been so small—everyone is connected to everyone through the Internet, social media, email,

YouTube, while air travel brings people from around the world together faster than we could ever imagine. While the world changed before we were on the face of the earth and will continue to do so after we are gone, we Christians who live on the earth now have a limited time to connect with our neighbors. For us, it is time to look at how we do evangelism in this changing world, in particular with our newer neighbors. In fact, it is overdue. Psalm 90:12 asks the Lord to teach us to number our days so that we might have a heart of wisdom. The world is changing rapidly. How do we as instruments of God for the spread of the gospel gain biblical wisdom for these fast-changing times? It is all so complex, but when we look at one immigrant and refugee family, it all changes.

We should note that this book is personal for both of us. For me (Eugene), not a week goes by that I'm not reminded of my story as an immigrant. Now, of course, I know that my core identity is rooted as a child of God, but our experiences play a part in the way we see our world, and for me, the story of immigration is one of the primary lenses.

I'm reminded of the story of parents who experienced unfathomable hunger and poverty. I carry within me their stories of fleeing what is now North Korea before the Korean War broke out. I carry with me the story of my father, who, only recently at the age of eighty-two, shared with me for the very first time the part of his story where he lived in a refugee camp—separated from several members of his family. When I asked him why he had taken so long to share that part of the story with me, he answered, "Some things are too painful to share."

Indeed. There are pain and trauma in the story of immigrants and refugees. But there are also incredible courage, faith, and perseverance. This is also part of my story. I am moved by the courage and tenacity of my parents. And while I also experienced my share of prejudice, racism, and barriers, I've experienced God's mercy, grace, and love in very tangible ways through the people of God. Again and again I have encountered believers—even in all their imperfections—who seek to embody what they believe as followers of Christ. I invest in this book as a tribute to my parents and to the many that demonstrated the radical love and hospitality of Christ. And, yes, we write this book out of our love for the church today—a body that at times feels like it's lost its footing in the chaos and craziness of our polarized, political world where it seems as if more and more Christians are in a space where their politics inform their theology rather than their biblically rooted theology informs their politics.

My (Samira's) family and I are similar to Eugene and his family. As a Muslim-background believer whose family is persecuted, I completely understand the complexities, frustrations, fear, and even hatred toward those we perceive as enemies of the gospel. I get it. As a refugee, I also understand firsthand the challenges refugees and immigrants face in a new country and how significant the work of the church in the lives of refugees and immigrants can be. I am a church mobilizer. As a missionary, I started a ministry in Dallas, Texas, called Gateway of Grace that rapidly grew and, today, is in partnership with close to one hundred churches and Christian organizations. Since starting Gateway of Grace in 2011 as a cross-denominational church-mobilization ministry, I have learned a substantial amount about the obstacles of ministry to refugees and immigrants. Migration and refugee resettlement patterns are very significant to the evolving formation of our society, as well as to the well-being of the church. Texas, for example, has historically been the largest hub for refugees in the United States, receiving thousands every year.[2] What does that have to do with the church? At the inauguration of the temple in Jerusalem, in 2 Chronicles 6:32–33, Solomon prayed a beautiful prayer: "Likewise when foreigners, who are not of your people Israel, come from a distant land because of your great name, and your mighty hand, and your outstretched arm, when they come and pray toward this house, may you hear from heaven your dwelling place, and do whatever the foreigners ask of you, in order that all the peoples of the earth may know your name and fear you, as do your people Israel, and that they may know that your name has been invoked on this house that I have built." It reminds us that even while we work to meet the many pressing needs of foreigners, refugees, and immigrants, the heart of God's will is that they may know the name of the Lord. This matters to the church. As the great theologian Hans Urs von Balthasar, in *A Theology of History*, reminds us, "The Christian and the Church attain to their true essence, their *eidos*, which exists already in Christ the Bridegroom, insofar as they receive and keep in themselves the will of the Father." He goes on to say that the will of God is "the seed of grace, which is always both the seed of mission and, for that very reason, at the same time a seed of formation and development."[3] This book is written in light of this understanding of God's mission, including the mutual relationship between the church and refugees, immigrants, and the poor. As we serve and share God's grace, we mature into the whole measure of the fullness of Christ (Eph. 4:11–15).

In my own ministry, my passion for the maturity and missional well-being of the church puts me in front of people of diverse denominations with diverse political and social backgrounds. As you can imagine, after each speaking engagement or workshop, people approach me and express concerns they would not feel comfortable expressing publicly. It is an honor to help my brothers and sisters in Christ see the biblical point of view and think through some of their unknown fears and even prejudices, and to mobilize them to serve God's mission for the salvation of the world. This book answers many of the questions I regularly receive about refugees and immigrants and our role as Christians in relationship with them.

The editors of this volume and its contributors feel that this is a unique time in history, in which evangelism itself is changing. Why is that? In the traditional pattern of mission and evangelism, Western missionaries are sent into other countries to fulfill the Great Commission and share Christ's love in practical ways with the world. What we are seeing now is a new work of the Spirit. While the patterns of migration and refugee resettlement can be explained factually using social and political sciences, the Christian must look above and beyond and seek the purposes of God amidst these facts. In light of the sovereignty of God, why are refugees and immigrants brought to our doorsteps? Acts 17 and the movement of people throughout the Scripture remind us that it is God who moves the peoples of the earth to fulfill God's purposes, which include seeking God and finding God. This does not mean that God brings about evil or injustice to accomplish this movement but rather that God is at work even in the tragedies and brokenness of the world to use them for good. In our time, we see God bringing the nations here, perhaps because of the freedom of expression and worship. In Iran, for example, it is illegal to convert from Islam to any other religion, and converts to Christianity face severe persecution, lose their jobs and property, go to prison, and experience torture and even rape. People come from countries in Africa, Asia, and the Middle East, where it would be extremely dangerous and costly to send missionaries. What does God want to do in the lives of vulnerable refugees and immigrants?

As Christians and ministry leaders who are passionate about reaching people from different nations with the good news of Jesus Christ, we find it hard and even painful to put in one sentence the words "evangelism" and "hurt." Our pain, however, does not change the reality of some people's negative and hurtful experiences of being evangelized in the United States as well as natives in countries where Western missionaries have been active. This is not even unique to evangelizing foreigners. We all have stories, from our churches, Christian media, and other platforms, about how individuals were hurt by the way they were evangelized. Prosperity gospel preaching has distorted the gospel into a "Jesus for Santa" campaign. The sinner's-prayer approach reduces salvation from the grace-filled conversion and transformative faith to saying yes to a one-line statement, usually under emotional pressure. False faith-healing practitioners take advantage of the misery and suffering of people who are desperate and manipulate them into saying yes to Jesus in order to be freed from their suffering. Examples of hurtful evangelism abound. Our hope and prayer are that we can have an honest discussion about our faithfulness, awareness, practices, and soundness of evangelism.

In writing this book, the first and foremost matter for us is the Bible. Biblical authority is what gives us the conviction and the courage to speak up on the most significant call we have as Christians, evangelism; it is a call that is often misused and abused. The Bible not only gives us the determination to speak up but also provides us with answers about biblical evangelism and many an example. The clarity of the Bible on some of these matters can also help to remove doubt and argument from our discussion.

This book is concerned about the evangelism of immigrants, and refugees in particular. We are in the midst of the largest mass migration in human history. According to the United Nations High Commissioner for Refugees, there are 70.8 million forcibly displaced people in the world. To put this into perspective, this means we currently live in a world where nearly one person is forcibly displaced every two seconds as a result of conflict or persecution. If we believe in the authority of the Bible and the sovereignty of a God who moves the families of the earth, the questions, for the believer, are: *What is God up to? How can I be a part of it? How can I equip myself to respond in godly and faithful ways to suffering and displaced people?* This book is about helping us, together, to pray and consider some of the related issues in these questions.

Our hope and prayer are that this book will bring us closer together as Christians in our understanding of the shape of God's mission in our tumultuous world and the ways in which we can participate in it.

1

EVANGELISM AND THE WAY OF THE CROSS

Andrew F. Bush

As the cold and gloomy day slipped into night, a chilling wind blew through the streets of Greenwich Village in Lower Manhattan. Late February still held enough of winter to blow New Yorkers to shelter. With not much more than spare change in my pocket, the best I could find was a fast-food eatery. The counter was open to the sidewalk, but there was some warmth from the grills. A fifteen-cent cup of hot coffee was its own comfort. Coffee was cheaper in 1972.

Sensing the presence of someone hovering behind me, I jammed my wallet deeper in my jeans pocket. Then someone said, "Excuse me. May we talk to you?" Swiveling on my stool, I faced two teenagers. They looked like they were fifteen or sixteen years of age. Before I could ask them to leave me alone, the taller one spoke:

"May we ask you a question? Do you know where you will spend eternity?"

Flustered by this abrupt question, I shot back, "What? Who does?"

"You can know where you will spend eternity if you put your faith in Jesus," he answered. "But you have to believe in him. The Bible says that whoever believes in him will not perish but have everlasting life."

Okay, I thought to myself. We are talking about religion. I needed a religious answer. "I grew up in church. I'm not into that now," I said with enough contempt that I hoped they would be on their way.

No such luck.

The same fellow pressed on. "You can have a new life if you receive

Jesus as your Lord and Savior. We could stand here all day and tell you about Jesus . . ."

"It's night. And it's cold," I protested.

". . . but you will only know how good believing in Jesus is if you receive him yourself."

With their chance to drive home their witness quickly slipping by, the other young man tried to close their witness convincingly. He said, "It's like drinking a cold glass of lemonade on a hot summer day. We could tell you about it, but if you had never tasted it yourself, you wouldn't really know how good it is."

It was a strange metaphor for a cold night. "Okay, okay," I said. "Thanks for your concern. But I'm going to finish my coffee."

I started to turn away, but one of the guys quickly pulled out a small pamphlet from his jacket pocket and extended it toward me. "Please take this and read it," he implored. It said something about "Salvation in Jesus" on the cover. Hoping to end the conversation, I took it as nonchalantly as possible, slipping it quickly into my pocket. The dauntless young witnesses for Jesus wished me well and headed out into the night.

That was unusual, I thought to myself. I had been witnessed to by two street preachers. Well, it was New York City. You bump into all kinds on its streets.

Later that evening in the apartment where a friend was letting me couch-surf, I pulled the gospel tract out and looked it over. On the cover was a silhouette of Jesus. Inside was a list of Bible verses. On the back was a short prayer that urged the reader to ask God to make the love of Jesus real to him or her.

Alone that night, I slipped onto my knees. Perhaps it was the sincerity of the young Christian witnesses. Perhaps it was my gnawing loneliness that could not be suppressed. Whatever the reason, I prayed for the love of Jesus to be made real to me.

Two years would pass, but that prayer was answered. I was living among counterculture fellow travelers in northern New Mexico who had dropped out, leaving their college studies, as I did, or uptight jobs in the cities. From outward appearances I was as far removed as one could be from the strictures of religion. I would soon discover I was not out of reach of the love of God.

In my journeys, another witness for Jesus had given me a Bible. I had stuffed it in the bottom of my backpack, where it was largely forgotten. One day, for some reason, I pulled it out and started to read. Its words seemed to come alive. Who was this amazing man, Jesus, who both spoke words of forgiveness and called people to forsake their sin (John 8:11)? After several months of contemplating the life of Jesus, the love of God came flooding into my life. The revelation of that love broke through the fog of my confusion. The love of Jesus melted my stubbornness. I became a follower of Jesus. Forty-five years later, Jesus remains as beautiful, radical, and authoritative to me as on that first day.

A Legacy of Witness

Street preaching, distributing gospel tracts to strangers, is probably the most ridiculed form of Christian witness. Such activity is reckoned to be rude, intrusive, fanatical, and ineffective. Can someone who accosts strangers in public places and challenges them to make a decision to believe in Jesus on the spot be taken seriously? How can God be involved in anything so apparently foolish?

Those young men in New York City had no way of knowing it, but in spite of the apparent futility of their efforts, they sowed a spiritual seed in my life that would bear fruit in God's time. They also were continuing the long line of women and men who have been witnesses of God's salvation through Jesus Christ that began with the first believers in Jesus as recorded in the book of Acts and continues to the present.

A brief overview of the heritage of today's evangelism should begin with Peter, the wavering apostle who denied the Lord Jesus three times after the arrest of Jesus (Luke 22:54–62). By the force of the reality of the resurrection of Christ Jesus, Peter's doubt was replaced by faith. The reality of Christ's resurrection was driven home to Peter by a large haul of fish that apparently materialized at Christ's command. From that same catch Christ Jesus cooked a breakfast of fish for Peter and the other fishermen on the Galilean shore (John 21:1–14). Jesus had risen indeed!

Before he ascended to heaven from the Mount of Olives, the resurrected Jesus promised his followers that the Spirit of God would be given to them. Furthermore, when the disciples of Jesus received the power of God through the Spirit, Jesus said they would be his witnesses to the farthest reaches of the world (Acts 1:8).

A few weeks later, on the Jewish feast day of Pentecost, the Spirit of God did indeed dramatically fall upon the disciples who were praying in Jerusalem (Acts 2:1–8). Emboldened by the Spirit, Peter stood up and proclaimed the first public evangelistic message of the Christian community. He declared that Jesus, who had been crucified, had risen from the dead. This remarkable account describes the result of Peter's evangelism: "Now when they heard this, they were cut to the heart and said to Peter and to the other apostles, 'Brothers, what should we do?' Peter said to them, 'Repent, and be baptized every one of you in the name of Jesus Christ so that your sins may be forgiven. . . .' Those who welcomed his message were baptized, and that day about three thousand persons were added" (Acts 2:37–38, 41).

Three thousand people accepted Peter's message of the *euangelion*,[1] the good news of salvation in Jesus! This was the first example that "God decided, through the foolishness of our proclamation, to save those who believe" (1 Cor. 1:21). The emerging community of believers in Jesus as the Savior and Lord, with its burning passion to communicate the good news, continued to grow.

Remarkably, when the first Christians were scattered from Jerusalem because of persecution, the Bible says they "went from place to place, proclaiming the word" (Acts 8:4). The canonical Gospels of Matthew, Mark, Luke, and John had not yet been written. What did they proclaim? Certainly, it was this central message of the forgiveness of sins and of eternal life that there is in faith in Jesus Christ. How wonderful it would have been to hear those first evangelists! They were ordinary folks—women, men, and perhaps even some children—who had experienced new life in Jesus.

Then, in one of the greatest conversions of the twenty centuries of Christianity, Saul, the man who had led the persecution of the Jerusalem church that caused Christians to flee, had his own encounter with the glorified Christ Jesus. What an encounter it was! While Saul was on his way to arrest Jewish followers of Jesus in Damascus, bright lights shone from heaven and Jesus spoke aloud, "Saul, Saul, why do you persecute me?" (Acts 9:1–19). Saul was smitten in conscience and brought to repentance and faith in Jesus Christ.

Saul, better known as the apostle Paul, more than any of the first disciples, became the one who paved the way for the gospel to be shared with gentile nations. His passion for the *euangelion* became the driving force of his life. He declared in his letter to the believers in Rome that he was "a servant of Christ Jesus, called to be an apostle, set apart for the gospel of God" (Rom. 1:1). Paul declared that he would adopt whatever lifestyle would be necessary so "that I might by all means save some. I do it all for the sake of the gospel, so that I may share in its blessings" (1 Cor. 9:22–23). He sought to pass on this same zeal to his disciples, such as Timothy, whom he exhorted to "do the work of an evangelist" (2 Tim. 4:5).

The Dramatic Spread of the Gospel

In the first two centuries after Christ, the fervor to share the good news of God's salvation in Jesus caused the steady spread of the Christian faith throughout the Roman Empire and beyond. Early followers of Jesus not only declared a message, they also conveyed through radical acts of servanthood the humility and the love of Jesus for all people. Historians describe that when the plague struck a city, causing its inhabitants to flee to the countryside, Christians intentionally went *into* the cities to care for the dying—and often died by their side. Unwanted newborns, thrown onto the public garbage heap to die of exposure, were rescued by Christians, who raised them as their own.[2] Even callous citizens of Rome were moved by the faith of devout Christians who gave thanks to God while being torn to pieces by wild beasts in the public arena.[3]

Such faith and witness won followers for Christ in all sectors of society in the Roman Empire. Three hundred years after Christ, it is estimated that one of every ten citizens in the empire—or about five million people—was a Christian![4]

Since those first centuries, the Christian faith has spread throughout the world as women and men, gripped with the same fervor, proclaimed the good news of God's salvation through Jesus Christ. Some of the most notable evangelists along the way include Patrick, who evangelized Ireland in the fifth century; the brothers Methodius and Cyril, who translated the Bible into Slavic languages in the ninth century; Francis of Assisi, who took the gospel out of the church and monastery and into the streets of Italy in the thirteenth century; and the Moravian community of Herrnhut in Germany, which prayed around the clock for one hundred years in the eighteenth century. Herrnhut became the first Protestant community to intentionally send out missionary teams to share the gospel in far-flung lands. John Wesley, it is reported, rode 250,000 miles on horseback to spread the gospel throughout England in the eighteenth century. The nineteenth century was an era of dramatic global expansion of the Christian faith. Important gospel messengers included evangelist Phoebe Palmer in the United States, Ann Haseltine Judson in Burma, and Charlotte "Lottie" Moon in China.[5]

Billy Graham was one of the most influential Christians in the twentieth century. He preached the gospel face-to-face to more people—210 million, including satellite feeds—than perhaps anyone in history.[6] He was a major catalyst for evangelism. At an international conference on evangelism in Amsterdam in 1983, Graham declared that Christians should "preach the gospel with urgency; preach it for decision. You may be speaking to some people who will hear the gospel for the last time. Preach it to bring your hearers to Jesus Christ."[7]

This cry for evangelism represents the core value of evangelical Christians, who celebrated Billy Graham's evangelistic "crusades" as high points of their movement. In the same effort to have as many people as possible hear the gospel of salvation in Christ Jesus, D. James Kennedy, a Presbyterian minister, founded Evangelism Explosion International in

1974.[8] This program trains laypeople to share the gospel. It has been used by thousands of churches.

What has been the result of these centuries of evangelism by both luminaries and rank-and-file Christians? Just as when Peter preached the gospel on the day of Pentecost and thousands received the message by faith and were baptized, the preaching of the gospel throughout the centuries has caused the dramatic global growth of the Christian faith. Although the majority of Christians in the world have resided in the West for several centuries, Christianity has become a vital, global movement. In fact, today more Christians reside *outside* of the West (Europe, Great Britain, and the United States) than within it. Christian communities in Africa, Asia, and South America are growing much faster than those in the West.[9]

Evangelism, from the apostle Paul to Billy Graham, has been central to Christian faith. Earnest Christians have lived and died to advance the gospel of Jesus in the world. So, is it reasonable to conclude that as Christians face the twenty-first century, they should continue to evangelize whenever and wherever possible? To answer this, we need to consider another scenario of attempted evangelism—and the possibility that evangelistic fervor can also hurt.

When Evangelism Hurts

Consider this hypothetical situation involving fictional characters.

Ahmad, his wife, Suhad, and two small children, Saleh and Imad, are Syrian Muslim refugees. They fled their home in Idlib in northwestern Syria when the city was rocked by the conflict between the Syrian army and antigovernment insurgents in 2017. The family miraculously survived a perilous sea crossing from Turkey to Cyprus. Ahmad and his family spent months in a barren detention center before they were given a visa to the United States.

Their immigration to the United States was in part facilitated by the fictional Christian Refugee Entry and Employment Diakonia (CREED). CREED workers met Ahmad and his family on their arrival at the Atlanta airport. They drove them to a furnished apartment near other resettled refugees. In subsequent weeks, CREED volunteers delivered prepared meals and helped drive Suhad and Ahmad to government offices to continue their immigration process.

Suhad and Ahmad were grateful for the kindness of the workers. They knew they were Christians. There was a reference to the Christian faith of the organization on its website. This did not bother this Muslim family. Some of their closest neighbors in Idlib were Christians.

The first weeks were difficult. Everything was different. The grocery stores were so big they felt dizzy in the long aisles. Some days they felt excited and happy with their new prospects; other days they were deeply discouraged. They had left all they had behind. They were experiencing the painful stages of adjusting to a new culture. Ahmad especially was finding it difficult to control his emotions.

Suhad and Ahmad were especially happy to learn that CREED was going to conduct a special children's program to help Syrian refugee children learn a few words of English and play some fun games. The leader would be Joe, an earnest twenty-five-year-old evangelical Christian. Joe had already gotten to know the families. He had transported them to appointments, helped deliver meals, and enjoyed conversations over the strong coffee he was offered in their homes.

On the first day of the children's program, the activities started nicely. Joe led the five-, six-, and seven-year-old kids in a game to learn important English words. "My name is ——," "I am five years old," the children said as a ball was passed around the circle. The parents who sat in the back whispered the new English phrases and laughed at each other's mispronunciations.

After a break for refreshments, there was a curious change of direction in the activities. Crayons were distributed, and the Syrian children started coloring an image of Jesus. The caption of the coloring pages read "Jesus loves the little children." Red, yellow, and blue scrawls and swirls began to fill the pages. The parents looked at each other. In Islamic faith, images of the prophets are discouraged.

When the last children finished coloring, Joe gathered them in a circle and asked, "How many want to pray?" Three of the kids raised their hand. A few of the parents looked uncertainly at each other. Joe pushed ahead. "Let's pray," he said. Bowing his head, Joe began, "Dear Jesus . . ." Then suddenly—

"What is this?! Stop!" a Syrian refugee parent almost shouted. "It is *haram* (forbidden) to pray to Jesus." Suhad glanced at Ahmad, whose jaw was clenched in anger. Ahmad spoke up, "We bring our kids here and you take advantage of us in this way? We thought you were good people. Are you crazy? We are Muslims. It is not permitted to pray to anyone but Allah." The parents swiftly gathered their kids and departed. A few threw the child's coloring project in the trash. The rest left them on the tables. The day was a total disaster.

Joe was shocked. He wasn't trying to evangelize . . . exactly. Well, if he was honest with himself, perhaps he did want the activities to move the kids and the parents toward accepting Jesus as their Lord and Savior. He wanted to bless the refugee families. What is a greater source of blessing than knowing Jesus is Lord? he reasoned.

The following day Ahmad called the program's director to state that he was very upset with the relief group, and that his family would look for help elsewhere. All the other Syrian Muslim families withdrew from cooperating with the relief agency as well.

Evangelism and Power

What is the problem in this scenario? Some might conclude that the problem is the unbelief of the Muslim families; the refugees needed to repent and believe in order to truly know God. Besides Joe's obvious lack of knowledge about the faith of the Muslim refugees, the problem is that Joe was using his position, which was empowered by his control over the resources the Syrian refugees required, to take advantage of the neediness of the families. He was using his position to impose what he knew to be a blessing on the families, who had a different belief system. In short, he was taking advantage of his position to evangelize the children and the parents. When some means of leverage is applied with evangelism—or any type of ministry—it becomes abusive. It ceases to represent Christ.

Perhaps this hypothetical scenario is too obvious. If Joe had even a modicum of awareness that Muslims regard prayer to any being other than Allah the most serious sin, would he really have tried such a ham-handed approach as to pray with the children? Well, perhaps not; however, Joe could have abused his position even more egregiously.

In any event, the temptation of Christians to use some type of power to evangelize has plagued efforts to make Christ known through the centuries. Just as there have been noble attempts to share the gospel of Jesus in humility and integrity, as mentioned previously, so there have been efforts to compel conversion to Christ. At times this use of power has been severe; at other times the use of pressure has been unintentional, an expression of Christian culture that has become deeply enmeshed with sources of influence in society.

During the Inquisition in Spain in the fifteenth century, Jews who did not convert to the Christian faith could be killed. Many fled to safety—in Muslim lands! In modern Protestant missions since the end of the eighteenth century, power has been applied more subtly by merging invitations to become Christian with access to education, health care, travel, food, etc. This is what the missions leader Samuel Escobar has termed "imperial missions."[10]

Why do imperial missions and evangelism coexist? One reason might be that Christianity's privileged alignment with wealth, political influence, etc., has deep roots in Western society.[11] This entanglement with sources of social privilege has so deeply formed Western Christianity that it has become normative and assumed. Many American Christian workers like Joe have been discipled with American Christianity's alignment with social influence as part of the warp and woof of their Christian culture. For example, such Christian culture takes for granted that Christian prayers should predominate at a public ceremony during a time of national distress, or that elected public officials should openly confess their faith.

Joe's predicament as a Christian worker who desires to help the practical needs of refugees but also to share the good news of salvation in Jesus Christ raises important questions. Can Christians ever disperse resources that refugees, victims of natural disasters, or the poor need without the resources becoming a bait and switch to promote evangelism? Must relief workers abandon evangelism? If evangelism is so central to the life and continuation of the Christian faith, should the Christian community generally abandon social action in its various forms? If both are essential, is there a formula for how and when a Christian worker should employ one or the other? In answering, let us first consider social action and whether it is really something Christians should pursue.

The Kingdom of God and Social Action

Social action to relieve the suffering of the indigent or refugees is indeed a vital part of the work of the church to communicate the reality of the love of Jesus to the world. This mandate to bring holistic ministry that touches every part of people's lives, including their physical needs, is underscored by Jesus's emphasis on the kingdom of God. The Bible says, "Jesus came to Galilee, proclaiming the gospel of the kingdom, and saying, 'The time is fulfilled, and the kingdom of God has come near; repent, and believe in the gospel'" (Mark 1:14–15).

This term, "the kingdom of God" (*basileou tou theou* in Greek), can be translated as the authority or reign of God. It is by the authority of God that what has been damaged in the world by sin is repaired and made whole. Ultimately, God's plan to restore all things that are broken and hurting extends from our inner spiritual lives to our physical and psychological needs and to the broken values and institutions of society.

For example, immediately after proclaiming the good news of the arrival of God's delivering authority, Jesus demonstrated it in a new and radical way by healing, feeding, casting out devils, welcoming the outcast, and rebuking oppressive social habits (Mark 1:21–32; Luke 7:36–50). Jesus's whole life actualized the good news of God's freedom and restoration from all the effects of the fall of humankind.

Because the coming of God's authority into the world means that every facet of life can be redeemed and restored, responding to physical, spiritual, emotional, and psychological needs of people must be fundamental to the ministry of the Christian community. As Billy Graham wrote: "We communicate the Gospel by compassionate social concern. I believe that there is a social involvement incumbent upon us, and commanded in the Scriptures. Look at our Lord. He touched the leper! Can you imagine how that leper felt to be touched? The leper had to go around ringing a little bell and calling out, 'Unclean! Unclean!' Jesus touched him. Jesus was teaching, by example as well as by precept, that we have a responsibility to the oppressed, the sick and the poor. Sometimes that is the best way to approach them, touching them with our compassion."[12]

This seems reasonable, but not all are happy with the idea of social concern or action. While watching my granddaughters in a kickball game on a balmy evening in Santa Barbara, California, I began chatting with another grandparent. He was a Christian, and the topic of the interests of today's generation of followers of Jesus came up. I mentioned that for many Christian university students social justice is a high-priority concern.

The grandparent's immediate reply: "I hope not."

I was taken back by his brusque response. "Why do you feel so opposed to social concerns?" I asked.

"When liberals started pushing the 'social gospel,' many Christians stopped preaching the true gospel," he said.

This fellow's reaction is not unusual. Concern for social needs only amounts to "social work," as a West Virginia pastor said to me recently. For many Christians, the concerns of millennial and Gen Z Christians for social issues like human trafficking, refugee resettlement, homelessness, and other social crises represent a weakening of conviction in the verbal proclamation of the gospel of salvation in Christ Jesus. Didn't the apostle Paul state that "I decided to know nothing among you except Jesus Christ, and him crucified" (1 Cor. 2:2)?

The reason for the aversion of many evangelicals toward the "social gospel" and, conversely, for their commitment to the proclamation of the good news of God's salvation in Jesus is important to understand. In the early twentieth century, a deep division occurred between Christians who staunchly affirmed the divine inspiration of the Bible and those who were skeptical of such inspiration. The latter were also wary of evangelism, which requires a deep confidence in the Bible's message.

The rise of the theology of social responsibility coincided with the deterioration of confidence in the Bible as the authoritative, inspired Word of God. What could mission to the world be if a church or denomination no longer had confidence in the Bible's statements on human sinfulness, the need for salvation, etc.? Serving one's neighbor and addressing social concerns were reckoned to be a suitable substitute. After all, it was reasoned, didn't Jesus feed the hungry?

In 1917 Walter Rauschenbusch wrote a book entitled *A Theology for the Social Gospel* that reinforced this emphasis on social action as ministry. He argued that the concept of the kingdom of God preached by Jesus intends that God can redeem not just the individual from the guilt of sin but also institutions or structures in society that promote oppression of others through racism, economic injustice, and more.[13]

Conservative evangelical Christians who stressed the Bible as God's authoritative Word reacted strongly against this shift of emphasis in outreach from the verbal proclamation of the gospel to social action. "Social gospel" became the derogatory description of any ministry involved in responding to social needs, and that by implication also avoided the verbal proclamation of the gospel.

These contrary views resulted in the "fundamentalist" versus "liberal" split that divided churches, denominations, and seminaries. For most of the twentieth century, these battle lines remained. However, both evangelicals and Christians who emphasize a social agenda have begun to modify their positions. For evangelicals, the International Congress on World Evangelization in 1974 in Lausanne, Switzerland, was a critical step in this process of addressing the importance of social concerns.

At Lausanne, evangelical leaders from around the world gathered to ascertain the state of global missions and plan for their advancement.[14] At the conclusion of the congress, the Lausanne Covenant was ratified.

In this document, participants affirmed the importance of evangelism but also underscored the importance of social action. Article 4, entitled "The Nature of Evangelism," emphasizes the following:

> To evangelize is to spread the good news that Jesus Christ died for our sins and was raised from the dead according to the Scriptures, and that, as the reigning Lord, he now offers the forgiveness of sins and the liberating gifts of the Spirit to all who repent and believe. Our Christian presence in the world is indispensable to evangelism, and so is that kind of dialogue whose purpose is to listen sensitively in order to understand. But evangelism itself is the proclamation of the historical, biblical Christ as Savior and Lord, with a view to persuading people to come to him personally and so be reconciled to God.[15]

Immediately following this affirmation of the importance of evangelism, article 5, entitled "Christian Social Responsibility," states:

> Here too we express penitence both for our neglect and for having sometimes regarded evangelism and social concern as mutually exclusive. Although reconciliation with other people is not reconciliation with God, nor is social action evangelism, nor is political liberation salvation, nevertheless we affirm that evangelism and socio-political involvement are both part of our Christian duty. For both are necessary expressions of our doctrines of God and Man, our love for our neighbor and our obedience to Jesus Christ.[16]

The question then is, which has priority? The Lausanne Covenant is unambiguous. Article 6 states: "In the Church's mission of sacrificial service, evangelism is primary."[17] That conclusion is certainly affirmed by evangelicals who remain distrustful of social action. In their skeptical view, social action is only truly acceptable in outreach if it is accompanied by evangelism. A few years ago, my wife was visiting a large church in Denver, Colorado, to bring a mission report. She described her mission work as a midwife in Ramallah in the Palestinian Territories. The first question during the discussion time: "Of course, you do this in order to share the gospel, right?" In response, could not her midwifery work itself have been a witness of God's love to the Muslim community?

Beyond Formula: The Primacy of the Love of God

Let's return to the fictional account of Joe, his work with the relief agency CREED, and his missteps that offended the Muslim refugee parents. Joe's assumptions had been informed by the conviction that evangelism has primacy over social action. Furthermore, he had been convinced that social action needed to be justified by an accompanying effort of evangelism. After Joe's very difficult confrontation with the Muslim refugee parents, he and his supervisors discussed what steps they should take to guide their ministry to avoid future conflicts. The situation was serious. A major part of their work would now be curtailed because the Muslim families did not want to be associated with them.

In a daylong meeting, the leaders tried to arrive at a formula that would guide their dual obligations to bring relief and appropriate evangelism. They didn't want to use their relief efforts as leverage to present the gospel. That approach had clearly failed. At the same time, they did not want to lose any opportunity to share the gospel. What if we are the only ones with contact with the refugees who are willing to share the gospel? they wondered. They felt they needed a policy that could guide them in whatever situation might arise with refugees, but nothing seemed to be satisfactory. None in the group wanted to form a policy that would abandon evangelism.

How could these sincere Christians find a way to be faithful to their obligation as Christians to share the gospel of Jesus and to care for the hurting and the homeless? Perhaps a place to start is the wellspring of all ministry, the crucifixion of Christ Jesus. Are there principles that can be drawn from the example of Christ's death on the cross that can guide those concerned with both social action and evangelism?

The apostle Paul certainly draws a straight line between the crucifixion of Jesus and how we should conduct ministry. He writes to the Christians in Philippi:

> In your relationships with one another, have the same
> mindset as Christ Jesus:
>> Who, being in very nature God,
>>> did not consider equality with God something to
>>>> be used to his own advantage;
>> rather, he made himself nothing
>>> by taking the very nature of a servant,
>>> being made in human likeness.
>> And being found in appearance as a man,
>>> he humbled himself
>>> by becoming obedient to death—
>>>> even death on a cross!
>> Therefore God exalted him to the highest place
>>> and gave him the name that is above every name,
>> that at the name of Jesus every knee should bow,
>>> in heaven and on earth and under the earth.
>
> (Phil. 2:5–10 NIV)

The apostle exhorts us to have the same "mindset" or attitude that Jesus had. What is this attitude? Christ "made himself nothing," or, as the Greek word *kenōsis* connotes, Jesus "emptied" himself. He emptied himself, or voluntarily laid down his prerogative to glory as the Son of God, and willingly entered into the human experience, being "made in human likeness." In this act of joining us in our humanness, he affirmed the value of all humanity. Particularly, as we think of refugees and others in need, by laying aside his claims to power, Jesus identified with the weak and marginalized. In the crucifixion he affirmed their value.

We then, in order to have "the same attitude," must do the same. We must first affirm the value of those in need. This is done by identifying with the vulnerable in their weakness, standing by their side in solidarity, listening quietly to their stories. It is moving past the posture of the strong helping the weak. As one theologian remarks: "Identification with those on the periphery implies voluntarily laying aside power and status, or those privileges that separate us from the weak."[18] This surely suggests the voluntary laying aside of the assumed prerogative we have to share the gospel.

Perhaps in our fictional account of Joe, the Syrian families decide to give him a second chance. In another children's meeting, he asks the children to color pictures of their homes in Syria. He then asks the parents to tell their stories of fleeing Syria. Moved by Joe's sensitivity, one father, as he walks out the door, comments on how kind Christians are to them. Joe simply thanks him. Some months later the same father asks Joe to explain to him what Christians believe. The outcomes of both of Joe's hypothetical encounters reflect the real experiences of aid workers who have shared their experiences with me.

On the basis of Joe's second, more positive experience, perhaps CREED decides that the most important training they could give their volunteers is in spiritual formation. Following in the attitude of Jesus, who was willing to let go of the prerogatives of power, is not easy. Spiritual formation has been the most neglected aspect of Christian outreach in recent decades. A central aspect of the preparation of all seeking to share the gospel must be the intentional consideration of how one's life reflects the radical love of Jesus, who made himself weak or lowly to bring spiritual healing to the most vulnerable.

Affirming Evangelism in Weakness

Today, straightforward evangelism is increasingly muted. A skeptical society has caused the church to become increasingly defensive about sharing the message of God's salvation through Jesus Christ. An ethos of pluralism pervades American society. In critiquing evangelism, I do not want to surrender to the skepticism of the age. If evangelism is regarded as foolish to an increasingly secular society, it is good to recall the apostle Paul's declaration that "since, in the wisdom of God, the world did not know God through wisdom, God decided, through the foolishness of our proclamation, to save those who believe" (1 Cor. 1:21). So, bravo to the sister or brother who dares to say to a coworker: "Jesus died that we might have not only a more meaningful life, but eternal life." Bravo to the two young men who presented the gospel to me in New York City.

We cannot create a formula for how and when the message of God's saving grace in Christ Jesus is to be shared. Such debate leads to more futile formulaic attempts to be agents of God's love in the world. Rather, may our goal be above all to serve with the attitude of selfless servant-hood in the weakness and vulnerability of the crucified Jesus. If we walk in such love, will we take advantage of the refugees' plight and pressure them to believe the gospel? Surely not.

As the supplicant who came to Jesus cried out, "I believe; help my unbelief!" (Mark 9:23–25), may we also cry out, "Lord, I love the home-less, the refugee, and the immigrant. Help my insensitivity! Lead me in the way of the cross, in the way of servanthood in weakness!"

Christians who love the gospel of Jesus and are walking in servant-hood can help us learn how evangelism in the way of the cross may be lived. For example, after my conversion in New Mexico, an older friend named Vernon guided me in my new Christian life. For more than a year, on Friday evenings I would accompany Vernon as he visited men in the Santa Fe County Jail. Vernon displayed sincere kindness and empathy as he listened quietly to the painful stories the men told of their lives. If a prisoner inquired about spiritual things, Vernon would share a passage from the Bible and explain that a new life through faith in Christ Jesus was possible. This good man was an example of evangelism in the way of the cross. At the end of his life, he was eulogized as a friend of the broken. He was an evangelist who did not hurt but healed—his was a worthy life to emulate.

~~~ ONE PERSON'S STORY ~~~

In the summer of 2011, a ministry from North Carolina rolled into the western suburbs of Chicago in fifteen-passenger vans full of enthusiastic young adults, free T-shirts, and bags of soccer balls. Their second visit to the area, the following summer, was markedly different from the first, after local residents who had witnessed their ministry the year before initiated direct conversations with their leadership to express serious concerns. I was one of those neighbors, and I am writing this years later, but this is my best recollection.

This ministry appeared seemingly out of nowhere and without prior warning. The leaders parked their vans at apartment complexes in Wheaton and Glen Ellyn, where most of the residents were low-income immigrant and refugee families. They were quickly a hit with the kids in my neighborhood because the energetic leaders dribbled soccer balls and invited kids to join them. Within days, the kids were recruited to soccer camps held around the area. They had a blast. It was something new and exciting to do, and the leaders lavished them with attention between soccer drills and Bible stories and devotionals.

Not everyone was excited about the group's involvement in the community, however. On the first day of camp, parents discovered that their children were missing. The landlord fumed and called the police. Hours later, the vans returned and the kids tumbled out, sweaty and beaming from the fun they had had. But this ministry had recruited kids without talking to their parents, without explaining the soccer program or the organization, and without getting permission to drive the children outside of the neighborhood or do devotions. In many instances, the children were the only ones who explained to the parents where they had been, as they begged and pleaded to be allowed to go again the following day.

One of the kids was Vincent (not his real name), who was in junior high and a talented player. By the end of this ministry's stay in the area, Vincent had been invited to be a junior leader with the group and had attended more than one area camp, not just the one for the kids from his neighborhood. Then he was invited to return with the group to North Carolina to live with them for a year and to work on his soccer skills, to be discipled in the Christian life, and to attend public school there. Vincent must have been extremely flattered to be asked, and he begged his father to let him go. Vincent's parents were not Christians, and they were not eager to have their young son go halfway across the country to live with strangers. Vincent was so insistent, however, that after many conversations, Vincent's father relented. He acted resigned in his decision and indicated that this was the beginning of his son's coming of age and that he could no longer decide what was best for his son.

The same ministry returned to the area for a second summer in 2012. Christian neighborhood residents and a local pastor initiated at least three meetings with the group to express concern over the ministry approach. The group's leader apologized for the prior year's confusion and committed to talking with parents and getting permission for their kids' participation. They were made aware of local networks and churches already involved in the neighborhoods and were encouraged to partner together under local leadership.

Nevertheless, one landlord refused to let them return to his complex without an apology. For years afterward, that landlord continued to target any outside groups who came to his apartment complex and called the police on many of them.

Vincent attended school in North Carolina for a year, and presumably he made a profession of faith. When he returned home, he struggled in high school and was suspended for fighting. Eventually, he dropped out. Today, he lives at home with his family, a twenty-something with no high school diploma and no job. He has had a couple of run-ins with the law, and his parents have expressed to me their frustration that he sleeps all day, spends time with questionable friends at night, won't help with his little sister, and isn't willing to work. It is hard to say how much this has to do with his leaving his family and the influence of this ministry, but it does seem to have caused harm.

—*A concerned community member*

2

EVANGELIZING THE HURT AND TRAUMA

Issam Smeir

Khalid is a Libyan lawyer. In 2007 he was imprisoned after protesting Muammar Gadaffi's rules. In prison, Khalid was tortured for months before he was let go. While in prison, Khalid realized that many of his conversations with close friends were recorded and passed to the security apparatus in Libya and then used against him in interrogation. After getting out of prison, Khalid decided to leave Libya. He was broken physically and emotionally. More importantly, he could no longer trust anyone from his family or his friends. He also lost his faith in God. "How can a just God allow this to happen to an innocent person like me?" he used to ask himself. In Egypt, Khalid was invited once to attend a local church by an Egyptian man whom he met and befriended after moving there. Khalid was very suspicious at first, but he went anyway. His life changed as he attended the church. "It was hard at first to trust any person, but after a while I could regain my trust in people and ultimately with God," Khalid said. It was loving relationships that brought him to Christ, Khalid added. He was forever indebted to his Egyptian friends. They picked him from the ashes. Today Khalid is back in Libya and runs an NGO that works with traumatized children and women.

~~~

For the last twenty years, I worked as a mental health clinician serving children and adults who experienced trauma. My clients came from all backgrounds. Traumas, whether natural or man-made, affect all kinds of people. While many of my clients were refugees who survived civil wars and had to flee their native countries to either live in refugee camps or resettle in the United States, others experienced the natural traumas of hurricanes and tornadoes here in the United States. My clients were from different age groups as well. I worked with adult victims who experienced gang violence on the south side of Chicago and with children who were neglected and abused by their parents.

If there is a single word that describes my work, it is "stories." Most of the stories I heard were horrific. Women and girls told me of being sexually harassed or assaulted by trusted adults. Children told me they had to run for months through jungles away from war, violence, and wild animals. Adults cried as they told me how they were imprisoned for months and systematically experienced all kinds and forms of torture. Some of the families I worked with experienced division as family members ran away for safety or were abandoned.

Not all trauma stories that I heard had bad endings. I remember visiting a Kurdish refugee woman who was separated from her husband a decade earlier as each ran for safety during the war, to tell her that her husband had been located and was still alive. I will never forget the look on her face. Stories of triumph against all odds are common as well. I worked once with a single woman who made multiple bad decisions in her life. She had several children from different relationships and supported her drug addictions by prostitution. The woman turned her life to Jesus and was reunited to live with her younger children.

While some of my clients carried in their bodies reminders of torture and horrific events in the form of physical wounds, the masked psychological wounds to their souls were more painful, harder to heal, and way more debilitating. As a counselor, I have always thought about the role of the local church with those who have been afflicted the most among us. The body of Christ is supposed to be the safest place on Earth in times like these, a city on a hill and an oasis for healing. My favorite verse that I kept referring to is God's promise to those among us who have been afflicted the most.

> "He [God] will wipe every tear from their eyes.
> Death will be no more;
> mourning and crying and pain will be no more,
> for the first things have passed away." (Rev. 21:4)

It is that promise that I hold dear to my heart. I pray that you and I will be a part of it.

Trauma

Traumas—namely, events that involve danger of death, injury, or sexual violation—are on the rise. In 2019 there were 68 million refugees in the world, according to the United Nations High Commissioner for Refugees (UNHCR). That's the highest number of displaced people since World War II. According to the *UNHCR Resettlement Handbook*, posttraumatic stress disorder (PTSD) among refugees ranges from 39 to 100 percent.[1] Trauma is prevalent in the United States as well. Nearly a third of US youth ages twelve to seventeen have experienced two or more types of childhood adversity, according to a survey conducted by the National Survey of Children's Health in 2012. These traumatic events include interpersonal violence, accidents, and injuries that are likely to affect their physical and mental health as adults.

Traumatic events can come in different forms and types. The *Diagnostic and Statistical Manual of Mental Disorders (DSM-V)* lists four types of traumatic events that can lead to significant changes in people. These changes affect their functional level, might impair their productivity and lifestyle, and might disrupt important relationships. Traumatic events include experiencing life-threatening incidents, witnessing life-threatening incidents that happen to others, hearing in detail about distressing or life-threatening incidents that happen to close ones, and finally, long exposure to traumatic events, which is common among relief and first-responder workers.

Trauma and PTSD

The psychological reaction to trauma is called posttraumatic stress disorder (PTSD). The prefix "post-" means "after," so posttraumatic means the stress symptoms after the trauma. The concept of PTSD as a disorder started to attract medical researchers' attention after thousands of Vietnam veterans returned to the United States displaying psychological symptoms. Similar psychological symptoms were observed among women rape victims. The current definition of PTSD in *DSM-V* outlines psychological symptoms among survivors of trauma that consist of:

(a) intrusive thoughts that are quite evident as traumatized people uncontrollably play a videotape of vivid details of traumatic events over and over again. All of their attempts to get rid of scary images and sounds associated with the trauma fail.

(b) avoidance behaviors as traumatized people in an attempt to cope with their trauma actively avoid people, events, noises, smells and places that remind them of the traumatic event. Avoidance can be emotional as traumatized individuals typically have a difficulty in experiencing a wide variety of emotions, expressing their feelings toward other people, and subsequently may isolate themselves from others and feel less interested in enjoying activities that they used to like.

(c) alertness symptoms refer to an exaggerated startle response to events or reminder of the traumatic events. These symptoms result from an overall elevated level of alertness due to an enduring feeling of an anticipated threat. Traumatized people may experience frequent outbursts of anger and irritability. They can have problems staying focused during a conversation or during their job.

And finally (d) negative alterations in cognitions and mood. Following traumatic events, trauma survivors develop persistent negative and distorted beliefs and expectations about God, themselves and the surrounding world. These irrational thoughts develop negative trauma-related emotions such as fear, anger, guilt and shame that made survivors feel alienated from others. Thoughts such as the world is unsafe, and one should be very careful to trust others, are very common.

How Does Trauma Change Us?

PTSD is a disorder of the memory. Traumatic memories are typically referred to in the literature as hot memories.[2] They are fragmented but vivid in nature. They are also saved in a different format from other memories. Hot memories are activated automatically by cues or triggers and are associated with intense feelings of horror and helplessness, as if the trauma were recurring in the present. Once these memories are triggered, trauma survivors can experience a full-blown panic attack with symptoms that include increased heartbeat, fast breathing, high blood pressure, etc. Since these memories can occur at any time, trauma survivors learn quickly to avoid any potential cues—images, places, noises, thoughts, feelings, and such—that remind them of the traumatic event.

Trauma also changes the way people look at themselves, and most importantly, can cause long-term behavioral and personality changes. The most common request that I heard from my clients over the years was "Please help me to feel my old self again." That is because many trauma survivors divide their lifeline into two eras: pre- and posttrauma. Children and adolescents are more susceptible to long-term impact from being exposed to traumas. Not only are childhood years essential for kids to play and explore the world but, more importantly, these years are essential to learn how to attach emotionally to significant others. Traumas might produce long-term impairment to their ability to form healthy relationships in the future, ones built on the foundations of intimacy, commitment, and passion.[3] Moreover, the experience of trauma might produce very serious emotional problems, or emotional numbness, as many trauma survivors report restrictions in their emotional experience.

This impairment in experiencing emotions can explain the high correlation between PTSD and depression. Forty percent of PTSD patients display depressive symptoms on top of their PTSD symptoms, which makes treating trauma harder and more time consuming.

Spiritual Impact of Trauma

In addition to the physiological and psychological impact of trauma on the human body in the form of PTSD symptoms (*DSM-V*), trauma can have a significant impact on our souls. In fact, "trauma" is a Greek word that means injury to the soul. If spirituality can be defined as a person's private beliefs, and attitudes toward God, himself or herself, and the world, rather than overt behavior,[4] then there is a correlation between trauma and the human's spiritual wellness. Trauma shatters one's sense of feeling safe. It can also disrupt our belief system and alter our views about God as a loving creator, as in Khalid's life. Moreover, trauma can alter our views about other human beings and our world. It also can impact our feelings of self-worth. Often people who survive the trauma experience consistent feelings of guilt, self-pity, and shame.

Take, for example, the story of Tamar, recounted in 2 Samuel 13. Tamar was King David's daughter, and she was very beautiful. Her older brother Amnon developed such a pathological obsession about her that he became physically ill. Tamar was not married, and Amnon (half brother from a different mother) could have asked her hand in marriage from his father, King David. However, he, with the assistance of a wicked adviser, came up with a plan to lure her into his palace. Amnon pretended he was sick when King David came to check on him, and then asked his father to send his sister Tamar to come and take care of him while he was sick. Everything went according to plan, and when the two were alone, Amnon raped Tamar. After Amnon was done with her, he hated her so intensely that he asked his guards to put her out in a public manner to add insult to her injury. Tamar pleaded with him, but he refused. Tamar put ashes on her head and tore the ornate robe she was wearing. She put her hands on her head and went away, weeping aloud as she went. Tamar then went to live with her brother Absalom. The Bible describes her emotional state after the trauma.

This sad story is evidence that regardless of someone's status or wealth, extreme trauma combined with the lack of spiritual or relational support can be debilitating and can overcome any human's capacity to adapt. In this story, Tamar sadly did not have any support from her dad, King David; he was the only person who could have reinstated her honor publicly. Clearly the traumatic event changed Tamar significantly, as she felt alone and desolate. The impact on Tamar's soul and that of others who experience traumatic events can be felt and observed in the changes in their mood, particularly the increase in negative emotions such as fear, anxiety, guilt, and shame. These experiences are common among trauma survivors, as they tend to experience higher intensity and frequency of negative over positive emotions. Generally, fear is higher during the trauma than after the trauma, whereas other emotions—guilt, shame, and anger—tend to remain stable or increase posttrauma. Traumatized people are fearful the most during and immediately after trauma strikes, but with time fear decreases as survivors start experiencing a range of emotions, including guilt for surviving when others died; being ashamed of what happened to them; and being angry at perpetrators, at family members who did not protect them, or at God for allowing it to happen. While most trauma survivors experience these negative emotions, those who survive sexual assaults tend to report higher levels of posttrauma emotion than the other trauma groups.[5]

Evangelism and Trauma Healing

Evangelism means sharing the good news, and people who are traumatized are in desperate need of good news that brings them healing and restoration. Jesus said, "Come to me, all you that are weary and are carrying heavy burdens, and I will give you rest" (Matt. 11:28). Jesus also promises his followers peace. "Peace I leave with you; my peace I give to you. I do not give to you as the world gives" (John 14:27).

But can a faith journey with God in the form of a personal relationship bring healing and restoration to those who have been traumatized? The answer in the literature is yes. Walker et al. found that turning to God was an effective coping mechanism, and that trauma survivors who have faith gained a more optimistic perspective, and found greater meaning and purpose for their experience, than those who did not.[6] In that sense, a faith journey with God can bring hope, purpose, and meaning, especially when augmented by a community that provides social and spiritual support to those in pain. It is not only that the church community can be vital for those who experienced PTSD, but literature indicates that a supportive community such as the church can lower the risk of developing PTSD for those who experienced trauma.[7] In other words, members of empathic and supportive churches tend to develop fewer PTSD symptoms than those who experience similar traumas but do not have a similar support system in their lives. Belonging to a supportive church not only helps to heal trauma's wounds but also acts as a protective factor when trauma occurs.

Evangelism and sharing the good news can bring healing and restoration; however, as we reach out to those who are hurting, we must be aware that their vulnerable status might make them prone to coercion and manipulation. Those who faced recent trauma are more sensitive to any influence or pressure from others. Pressuring people who are hurting to make a quick decision to follow God or luring them by making false promises is immoral, ineffective, and harmful.

How Can Evangelism Be Harmful to Those Who Are Hurt?

1. By making false promises that their pain will disappear

Our good intentions to help those in pain can tempt us into rushing them to make quick decisions to surrender their lives to God. Our evangelical zeal can also push us to make false promises to them. A message that Jesus can heal their pain may or may not be a true statement. While accepting Jesus and belonging to a community of faith will help trauma survivors to cope with their trauma and pain, PTSD is a disorder, and people who display higher intensity and frequency of debilitating PTSD symptoms are in need of professional help. The danger of offering false promises and quick fixes is that those who profess faith after believing such claims might reject their newly found faith when life gets hard and their symptoms do not disappear. Instead, we are to tell people the gospel and that Jesus never promised an easy path but promised to be a companion during the difficult journey. Our evangelistic mandate is to share the gospel as it is and trust the Holy Spirit to open people's hearts to grasp Christ's redemptive work.

2. By confusing peace with comfort

Our evangelistic message should not promise hearers comfort. Jesus himself did not live a comfortable life, neither did he promise one to his followers. Instead, he promised peace to those who follow him. Unlike comfort, peace can coexist with pain and suffering. When we have peace in our lives, pain and suffering no longer take a central stage because they are placed in perspective when held up against a peace that surpasses human understanding (Phil. 4:7). This kind of peace is self-evident. It requires no sales pitch, no coercion.

3. By presenting an ethnocentric or nationalistic gospel message

A few years ago, I noticed that a Muslim refugee woman whom I knew previously started to attend services at our local church. When I saw her for the first time, I was surprised and excited. She was wearing her traditional dress, which includes a head scarf. Ms. Amal (not her real name) called herself a Jesus follower. She heard about our local church through a mutual American friend and decided to start attending. A few months later, Ms. Amal came to my office. She looked perplexed. She said that at our church's last service, her American friend leaned toward her at the end of the service, when the pastor was making a call to follow Jesus. Her friend whispered in her ear, "It is time for you to take off your head scarf." Ms. Amal, who was older, experienced several incidents of discrimination and persecution in her life, and for the past thirty years had worn her head scarf to convey modesty and not as a religious symbol. She was quite shocked and upset. She pointed out, and rightly so, that Jesus's mother, Mary, is shown wearing scarfs in all the icons she had seen. This woman felt that her friend was ashamed of the way she dressed, and she was disappointed, and I must say rightly so.

I do not believe the American friend acted with malicious intentions, but there was a hint of elitism that sneaked out and impaired her testimony. Our gospel message should never imply that our lifestyle, or our traditions based on Western culture, is superior to others; neither should it increase intentionally or unintentionally anyone's feelings of shame. Cultural sensitivity is particularly relevant and important as we interact and reach out to those who have experienced trauma in their past, as many suffer from a shame complex. Those people have perverted perceptions and assumptions about themselves and feel isolated and misunderstood. Our gospel message should counter these feelings by offering Christ's redemptive work that helps them to feel understood, valued, and loved by God and us.

4. By making evangelism task-oriented instead of relationally based

People who have been traumatized or abused might develop a fragmented sense of identity and a deflated sense of significance. The gospel message provides those who are hurting with a way to connect to God, who loves them unconditionally beyond man-made standards.

In the past twenty years, I have noticed that different cultures have different ways of bestowing worth on their members. Individualistic cultures in the West reward beauty, youth, accomplishments, and multitasking, while community-oriented cultures value hierarchy and loyalty to family and tribe. Regardless of the cultural background one grows up in, the value and worth of people are always conditioned. The good news has a unique message that traumatized people need to hear: their value and worth do not diminish because they are broken. God's love is always unconditional. In fact, God is closer to those who are broken.

The sacrifice acceptable to God is a broken spirit;
a broken and a contrite heart, O God, you will not
despise. (Ps. 51:17)

However, this can only be communicated effectively through meaningful relationships. And like all meaningful relations, effective evangelism can only be fostered with time and commitment. Traumatized people, particularly those who had been hurt or abused by people, may have trust issues. The question that looms constantly in their mind is: Why would you have good intentions toward me, and what makes you better than or different from all others who pretended to help me but had ulterior motives? These are valid questions that can only be answered through meaningful and healthy relationships that are built on trust. One way to form healthy relationships is to approach people with patience, love, and compassion. Effective evangelism in that sense is not a practiced task, but the message should be delivered within a loving relationship that is based on respect.

A few years ago, a newly arrived refugee family from Iraq got in trouble with the Department of Children and Family Services (DCFS). Legal custody was taken, and the children were placed in the foster system. The first two placements with foster families did not go well, and the two children were miserable. The family approached several other families from their community to keep their children, but all their requests were rejected. A Christian volunteer family with World Relief stepped in and offered to raise their children. The children were placed with them, and this family took good care of them. Both parents were happy with the level of care that their children were receiving with the family. One day the foster parents called the Muslim couple asking permission to take their children to church with them. The parents immediately accepted the offer. Three years later, the children are back living with their parents, and the foster parents still stop every Sunday to take these children to hear God's Word. When I asked the father how he feels about his children going to church with this family, he said he knows they have the best interest in their hearts for his kids. He trusts them.

5. By being transactional rather than transformational

We should never offer help based on the hearer's response to our evangelistic message, or as a reward for joining the local church. Many local churches fell into this mistake with good intentions in my native country of Jordan when local Jordanian churches tried to help Syrian refugees after the civil war started in Syria in 2011. Local churches, with the assistance of many Western churches, helped refugees with their basic needs, which is the right and moral thing to do; however, all the benefits were distributed after refugees attended services at the church. This unintentionally sent the wrong message to some refugees, who joined the church solely for the benefits.

The right approach is to love, help, and be compassionate regardless of how people respond to the gospel message. A Syrian Jesuit father once told me that his church in Aleppo distributed over 200,000 meals every day during the civil war without ever asking a question about the recipient's religion or denomination, or without ever asking anyone to attend church services. Even under heavy criticism from some of his church members, who complained that other religious organizations distribute donations exclusively for their own members, this Jesuit father stood firm. He told them, "There should be no religious test for our compassion."

Finally, people who are suffering and have experienced recent tragedy or trauma might be dependent on others for housing and food. Just because we have access to them all the time, that doesn't give us permission to invade their space and privacy. Evangelism is sharing good news and can't be intrusive. People need space and time to process their trauma. We need to be ready to share the good news with them, but we should always be aware and respectful of their boundaries. One should not negate the other.

Jesus's Paradigm of Reaching Out to Those Who Are Hurting

In Luke 10, Jesus tells the parable of the Good Samaritan. A man, a Jew, was abused and traumatized and left to die on the side of the road. While several good travelers passed on the opportunity of helping him, it was a Samaritan, a man from a different ethnic and religious group, who decided to reach out and help. Luke the evangelist, who is known for being attentive to details, mentions three things the Good Samaritan did that distinguished him from other bystanders.

First, he stopped. Stopping is an action more purposeful now than at any time before, as our current culture values productivity, multitasking, and efficiency. However, if we want to bring good news to those who are in pain, we need to make an intentional decision to slow down. Only then can we see and realize that they are in pain. This is particularly important, as many who are hurting choose to suffer alone. They even go around disguising their pain.

Second, the Bible says the Samaritan came closer. Nobody likes to look at pain face-to-face. Painful stories make us feel uncomfortable, and sometimes helpless. However, there is no other way to connect emotionally with those who are hurting than to get close to them. Coming closer means that we should be willing to listen more and talk less. Khalid, whose story is told above, recounted his first encounter with the Egyptian Christian who ultimately led him to Christ. "He treated me differently. As a refugee in a foreign land, you lose your dignity, but he listened, and believed my story."

Listening to those who have suffered can be hard, but only when we listen can we acknowledge that their pain is real and valid. This is important particularly because many trauma victims were told by perpetrators, or even by their families or friends, that their stories were fabricated, that their pain was not real. Listening to them will transform us from being bystanders to being witnesses. And as we witness what happened to them, we can share the good news to our brothers and sisters who are in pain, that they are not alone, that Jesus suffered and experienced injustice, and that he died on the cross not only for their sins but also for their sufferings.

The prophet Isaiah portrays the promised Messiah as the One who heals and encourages:

A bruised reed he will not break,
and a dimly burning wick he will not quench;
he will faithfully bring forth justice. (Isa. 42:3)

The allusion here is to people who are emotionally wounded—they look like a flower or plant with a bent stem, or a flame that is barely lit. They are bruised; they feel barely alive. They live behind fake smiles while inwardly they are in pain, barely alive, barely nourished, barely able to keep the light lit. Jesus carried not only our sins on the cross. Emotional healing was part of the work of the cross: grief, sorrow, and pain. One of the foundational verses for healing is Isaiah 53:5:

But he [Jesus] was wounded for our transgressions,
crushed for our iniquities;
upon him was the punishment that made us whole,
and by his bruises we are healed.

However, people who are hurting might not be ready to share their stories yet. When to share is a decision they should make. We only can tell them that when they are ready, we will be there to listen, to witness and affirm their worth and value.

Finally, the Samaritan reached out with compassion. When the Samaritan approached the injured man, unlike the others who moved away, he moved toward him with compassion. The word "compassion" has a Latin root that means to suffer together or suffer with. Compassion is one of God's attributes. His compassion is infinite and eternal. "His compassions never fail. They are new every morning" (Lam. 3:22–23 NIV). Jesus himself exemplified the Father's attributes, including his compassion. He wept at his friend's grave (John 11:35); he moved with passion when he saw the large crowd as sheep without a shepherd; and unlike the priests and teachers who did not associate with the common and neglected people, Jesus had compassion on them. He taught and loved them. When a Pharisee asked him about the greatest single commandment, Jesus gave two. Loving God

with all our heart, mind, and strength. Then he added a second commandment: to love our neighbors as ourselves (Matt. 22:34–39). To love our
neighbors as ourselves is the natural outcome of our love toward God.

When we suffer with people, we don't condemn them, we don't see
them as strangers. Instead we see them as the Good Samaritan saw the
injured man—as the beloved father of a child, a husband to a worried
wife, a brother, a precious son to a loving mother. In other words, we see
ourselves in that person. Compassionate evangelism transforms both the
evangelist and the hearer because the good news of Christ's compan-
ionship and love speaks to the brokenness and pain in both. It makes
evangelists a tangible manifestation of God's love and grace to share the
good news through words and deeds. At the same time, it transforms
the hearers who are hurting by referring them to a loving Savior, the
One who experienced and understands pain and suffering (Heb. 4:15). It
doesn't make hearers feel ashamed about who they are; it leaves the work
of conviction and sanctification for the Holy Spirit. A friend of mine
once told me when I invited her to attend our church, "I do not need to
go to a place that makes me feel bad about myself. Why would I go to a
church?" I felt sad and disappointed by her response, but there is a lot of
truth in what she said. Church was meant to be the safest place on Earth.
Jesus always demonstrated his love before telling people who he was. He
fed the hungry, healed the sick, and comforted those who were hurting.
He cried with them. Evangelism should always be conducted with compassion. In the words of Billy Graham, "We are the Bibles the world is
reading, we are the creeds the world is needing, we are the sermons the
world is heeding." True evangelism is joining Christ in his suffering to
give those who live in pain and misery a better life, for he came to give
us all a better life.

~~~ ONE PERSON'S STORY ~~~

A recent membership service at Gateway of Grace was a long time in coming for Leili, a former Muslim who converted to Christianity before leaving Iran eight years ago.

Leili was one of thirty-five confirmations and fourteen baptisms that occurred recently at Grace Community, a church plant of Gateway of Grace, led by Dr. Samira Page. Those baptized and confirmed as members came to Dallas as refugees from Bhutan and Iran. Many of those from Iran had converted from Islam, and those from Bhutan had converted from Buddhism and Hinduism.

Some of the confirmands from Iran were already Christian, like Leili, but had suffered persecution because it's illegal for Muslims to convert to Christianity there. She was arrested and jailed. Her daughter was only a few months old. Leili's husband spent a week in jail after authorities discovered him worshiping as a Christian in an underground house church. "They told my husband if you change religions, we can take your wife," Leili said. They were able to leave Iran legally, but they spent three years in Turkey as refugees under very difficult circumstances before coming to Dallas.

Gateway of Grace works to help with the practical, emotional, and spiritual needs of refugees. "It's a holistic approach. It's not a project," Page said. "We are meeting the whole person and the needs they have."

Coming to America as a refugee is challenging. Leili remembers crying a lot in the early days of living in a new country with a language she didn't yet understand. She felt extremely isolated and unable to care for the basic needs of her family. But through the ministry of Gateway of

Grace, she found herself surrounded by a loving community. Gateway of Grace helped her find a job, furnished her apartment, and purchased a car for her son so he could work. Little by little, Leili became self-sufficient, and now she works for Gateway of Grace in pastoral care, helping new refugees adjust to their new lives.

"The beauty of the ministry is that when these refugees get established, they start helping others by serving," Page said. "We create a culture in them that is conducive of service, not just receiving. That's a Christian value we place in their lives, regardless of their religion. They like these values, they see how good they are. Even if they don't become Christian, they pick up Christian values. And we see this as part of our work and witness too."

—*A grateful Christ follower and World Relief volunteer*

3

DOING EVANGELISM AS A CHURCH

Laurie Beshore

Mariners Church is a megachurch located in Irvine, one of the most affluent communities in Orange County, California. The area boasts people of high status and high income. The congregation mirrors the success of the surrounding community, and is filled with business leaders, entrepreneurs, doctors, professors, and lawyers. Early in the history of Mariners Church, it became clear to church leadership that serving people who are poor and in need was vital to the mission of the church. The danger for a wealthy church is the lure to become a country club for its members, and our church leadership wanted no part of that model. We were called to serve as Christ served, and what better place to start than our own surrounding neighborhoods?

Just fifteen minutes from Mariners Church, some of the poorest people in our county live in overcrowded, substandard housing, barely scraping by. Minnie Street, an impoverished inner-city area of Santa Ana, is home to a large population of immigrant families whose lack of access to education and limited English proficiency lead to low-status positions and barriers to better social mobility.

Proximity Changes Everything

It is shocking, really, to know that in the space of ten miles you can go from a megamansion overlooking the Pacific Ocean to a crammed single-bedroom apartment next to a railroad track, housing multiple families at a time. Yet, this is the reality of our community. The Bible says, "Since there will never cease to be some in need on the earth, I therefore command you, 'Open your hand to the poor and needy neighbor in your land'" (Deut. 15:11). This sentiment was echoed by Jesus: "You always have the poor with you" (Matt. 26:11a). The first lesson we learned about service is that proximity changes everything. We didn't have to look across the world for the poor, the marginalized, the immigrants, and orphans. We only had to look across the street. They were right there next to us.

Opening our eyes to the need in our community opened the hearts of people in the congregation to serve. Our initial approach to outreach was to offer events for the children of the community. There was no agenda. We just offered activities they'd not normally experience, like swimming and picnics. These were feel-good events, not really getting at deeper needs. In the end, the main purpose of these events wasn't life-change for the poor but an introduction for the members of our congregation to their "neighbors."

Our volunteers soon were drawn to these kids and their larger community. They wanted to engage with them in a more meaningful way. A small group of volunteers started tutoring the children of Minnie Street with their parents' permission. We'd caravan the kids from their neighborhood over to the church campus, about fifteen minutes away by car but drastically different in available resources. It amazed us how excited the students were to come for basic tutoring. The number of children wanting to participate grew each week. Many times, volunteer drivers would cram two or three kids to a seatbelt, transporting them illegally, because it was so painful to leave anyone behind. We of course do not recommend this, but we were coming to care deeply for these children and their families. We had to find a way to close the distance between us and them. Both in miles and in relationship, proximity changes everything!

Changing the Definition of Success

We began to explore the idea of opening a learning center on Minnie Street. One afternoon I met with a central figure in the neighborhood. Isabella (a pseudonym to protect her privacy) had lived in the neighborhood for several years and was clearly a highly respected member of the community. She spoke English well, which was invaluable to us because few of our team spoke Spanish, which, along with the Cambodian language Khmer, was the most commonly spoken language in the area. I asked her about an idea we'd been throwing around: What if we rented a couple of apartments in the complex where the families lived and opened a community center that would offer tutoring and a variety of other services?

To my surprise, Isabella was not at all enthusiastic about the idea. Her initially warm demeanor grew cold as she told me about the many people who had come to the community, preaching through a megaphone before dropping off bags of food and disappearing. They told the people how "loved" they were but never engaged in any meaningful way with the families. They rarely returned. There was no dignity in the interaction, only distance created by ignorance and fear. These outreach efforts, though perhaps well meaning, were misguided. How could you care about a neighborhood if you didn't stick around long enough to get to know the families? She felt these types of encounters did more harm than good.

I reminded Isabella that at that point we had a ten-year history of community engagement with her neighbors and investment in the community. We did not simply drop off food and leave. We'd provided tutoring, mentoring, and special events. We had gained the trust of many of the families. While at times it felt random, our hope was to become more strategic and consistent. We wanted to build a partnership with the people, and we hoped that was what the people wanted as well.

Isabella then cut right to the heart of the matter: the neighborhood was mostly Catholic, and the people didn't want to come to our church. For her, and for many in the community, there was a clear distinction between the Catholic Church and any other Christian faith. She was expressing an underlying suspicion that teaching kids to read wasn't our true aim, but that making our own church bigger was our actual goal. She felt we were out to change them. She made it clear that the neighborhood wanted no part of that sort of arrangement.

It was her turn to be surprised when I said we weren't hoping to make the residents of Minnie Street members of Mariners Church. This was a delicate time in our relationship, because there had been a history of hurts in the community. I think there can be a fear in creating faith-based outreach ministries, both for those serving and for those served. It has been done so poorly so often, even with the very best of intentions. People have been wounded by inappropriate uses of power and privilege. We are not immune to these mistakes. One thing we have learned from years of outreach ministry is that when you lead with money, there is often an underlying belief that you have control. Power and privilege often blind us to our own assumptions and become barriers to relationship.

One way the people we serve have uncovered our blindness happened through ministry to the local homeless population living in low-budget motels. These severely impoverished families lived in a motel room for three weeks at a time, but one week a month they were forced to move out so that the motel was not legally considered an apartment. Whole families shared a single room. The lucky ones had a hot plate for preparing canned meals. They were quite literally one step above living on the street.

Wanting to honor these families, and to provide the children with amazing experiences, we would throw big parties for them each month. Our initial goal was to create relationships with people right in our own backyard whose needs were beyond what most of our congregation could begin to imagine. We came up with what we thought was a brilliant idea: at parties we would use different colored name tags to identify who was a volunteer and who was a guest. Though their tags didn't say "homeless," they might as well have. Something we thought signaled respect for the people we served actually separated "us" from "them," and everyone knew it. Instead of inviting our guests to share equal footing in the relationship, we were quite literally labeling them as having lesser status. And we couldn't see it.

In all honesty, the people who benefited most from the parties were our church members. We were starting to see more clearly the divide between rich and poor, and to learn that there really was a greater need in our community than we had ever noticed. Parties came and went, but they didn't get us any closer to truly knowing one another as people. We were frustrated in our attempts to create meaningful relationships, and we couldn't understand why. Hadn't we given them the best we had to offer?

One day, a mother from a motel family asked, "Can I help arrange the parties? I will need a blue name tag." That small request for a name tag, and the underlying, bigger request to be identified as one who serves, opened our eyes. It was the beginning of a change in our philosophy of outreach ministry.

It turned out that our parties (and by extension our relative wealth) were not the best we had to offer. People don't want a handout, they want dignity. The motel families already felt worthless. They had been told over and over again how little value they had. Being labeled as a handout recipient only reinforced that feeling. They wanted to believe they had something to contribute, while our choices were about maintaining a sense of control over the line between us and them. That is not to say that we were being purposefully arrogant. We failed to see the very real divide created and maintained by our own material privilege.

Working with the motel families, we began to see a change in our definition of ministry success. We asked ourselves, what would be signs that the ministry had accomplished something worthwhile? For someone who has been in need, a sign might be to become someone who serves. For someone who has all material needs met in abundance, it might be recognizing that the only worth that matters is found in Christ. We started to realize that the definition of ministry success is when those who have little can worship and serve beside those who have much, each recognizing that our worth and significance are found in Christ alone. This understanding was so powerful, it became part of our outreach ministry mission statement.

Transparency Builds Trust

As we were moving toward partnership with the people of Minnie Street, the conversation I was having with Isabella about faith was both un-comfortable and necessary. She was honest with me about the fears the neighbors had about us coming into their community. They had been hurt by well-meaning people of faith, just as we had blindly hurt the motel families through our labels. I also needed to be transparent with Isabella, even if it put our budding relationship at risk. The truth is that it is our faith that differentiates us from being just another social service, and that would not change.

The way we have come to see outreach at Mariners, faith is never ma-nipulated, never forced, but is an important part of the relationship. Just like the parable of the sheep and the goats in Matthew 25, we are called to serve the poor, whether it brings someone to Christ or not, whether it is fun or it isn't, whether it is clean or it is messy. We are called to serve the poor. If we are whole and integrated in our walk with Christ, the light of our faith will come through in everything we do. Sometimes in actions, sometimes in words. This needs to be acknowledged and considered before a partnership is even considered. Hiding our light is just as manip-ulative as requiring people to accept our faith before we serve them.

I could not promise Isabella that matters of faith would not come up, because Jesus is the reason we serve. But I could promise her we weren't there to take away their faith or their culture. In fact, we would be honored to be given the opportunity to grow in relationship and get to know one another better as we created this learning center together. The relationship we envisioned was not meant to be one-sided. We hoped to become equal partners, working together to identify and eliminate the barriers between "us" and "them." When I told her this, Isabella cried. She said this was the first time a church group wanted to become part of the neighborhood itself.

The conversation set the tone for the relationship that has devel-oped over time: both sides openly and honestly sharing hopes, fears, and different points of view. Each challenging the assumptions of the other. Isabella set aside her initial fears and became the driving force behind organizing the neighborhood in the effort to open the first learning center.

Listening Is Key to Understanding

Once we had the blessing of Isabella as well as some other key stakeholders in the community, we were ready to begin in earnest. We knew that several groups had tried and failed to establish services in the community, and we were unsure what the key to success would be. To understand that, we had to talk to the community members. Our first task was to meet with several of the parents. We had to use translators for most of these conversations, as most of them didn't speak English well and very few Mariners volunteers knew a second language. We asked the residents what their biggest needs were but also asked about their dreams for their neighborhoods and their kids.

From there, community members broke into teams to interview their neighbors. It was important that the neighborhood stakeholders conduct the research for two reasons: First, they were more likely to get honest feedback. If a Mariners member had shown up on a doorstep, there would be a greater likelihood of guarded responses. And second, we wanted our stakeholders to know we were serious about not usurping their ownership. Each team had a yellow pad and a pen. They knocked on every door in the community, asking about needs and dreams.

If you had asked me what I thought the community center should provide, my list would have included a food pantry and perhaps even a clothing donation center right on site. Classes in budgeting and nutrition were an obvious must to me. We would bring resources to the people and then teach them to manage them. Certainly, that would make their lives better. I waited to see what the community would say, privately figuring that my ideas would ultimately rise to the top.

The teams came back with three great answers to our questions. First, the people wanted tutoring for their children. Most of the parents had not completed school, and since they were not fluent in English, they could not help with even elementary homework. Their youth were dropping out of school, unable to read and write in English, with no real job prospects. They wanted to offer their children a better future through education.

Second was developing English-language skills for adults in the neighborhood. They knew that if they were able to read and write in English, their job opportunities would immediately expand. Higher-paying jobs would allow them to better provide for their families. They didn't want a token handout; they wanted to gain the skills they would need to be successful in this society.

The third need was parenting classes. These families were losing their children to the gangs and drugs that infiltrated their neighborhood. They had no idea how to prevent it. In their home cultures, spanking or whipping was considered appropriate discipline, but in America they were accused of child abuse for the same parenting methods. They did not want to lose their kids to either the streets or social services, so they needed to learn some effective techniques for parenting that were acceptable in American culture.

What incredible priorities they had! Their priorities reinforced the inherent wisdom of the people of the community. These were the best things anyone could ask for, and I loved them all the more for asking for them. At the same time, their requests highlighted for me my own bias. My surprise that none of their top three requests involved us bringing money or gifts showed me that, deep down, I didn't think they'd be so insightful. I realized I didn't have very high expectations for them. I had underestimated the profound knowledge and understanding the people already had.

I realized that listening to what the community had to say about their needs was far more important than us telling them what we thought they should need. Had the learning center developed only with my own voice, or with the voices of the Mariners volunteers, it would have looked quite different. And it likely would have ended in another failed attempt to serve the people of Minnie Street. By listening first, we not only gained insight into the needs and hopes but we also gained respect for the people and their wisdom. Listening to their insights helped make our own blind spots visible, and further broke down the barriers between us.

From "Problem-Solvers" to Partners

With our goal lists in hand, we began meeting with the community leaders weekly. We discussed tutoring curriculum, facilities, and organization. We talked and talked, but in my mind, we never seemed to accomplish anything. Meanwhile, we had rented our first apartment, and it sat there empty. Anxious to kick-start some progress, I suggested that we stop meeting as a large group. My idea was to break into smaller teams that would each focus on different key issues. The stakeholders got quiet, but I failed to register the change in the room. It wasn't until the next week that I realized I had made a very big mistake.

The Mariners volunteers entered the meeting room to find that the community members had met early—without us. Instead of chairs arranged in a circle, as they had been in prior weeks, this week there were two rows facing one another. The residents occupied one row at the front of the room. On the blackboard behind them was written "Welcome Guest." We were, apparently, the guest. We had effectively been put in our place. They reminded us that this was their neighborhood, not ours.

My attempt at forcing a new structure on our meetings had been viewed as disempowering. As a group, they were very collective and community oriented. They were not interested in being split into separate groups, dividing their shared voice. For them, the larger group meetings were important for building relationships and learning to trust one another, even if it took longer to achieve our shared objectives. My drive to move toward measurable accomplishments undermined these important steps that needed to be taken at the pace of the neighborhood. I had seen only the problems that needed solving and missed the importance of building partnership.

The lessons in cross-cultural communication we learned at Minnie

Street were amplified on a global scale through our relationship with Pastor (now Bishop) Oscar Muriu, from Nairobi Chapel in Kenya. Several years ago, we took a look beyond our borders and noticed that while American churches were struggling to maintain membership, much less grow, Nairobi Chapel and churches throughout Africa were thriving. As my husband, Mariners' founding pastor and now pastor emeritus Kenton Beshore, said, "God is throwing a global party, and it's in the Southern Hemisphere." We knew we had to visit and find out what was going on there.

The ministry at Nairobi Chapel was exciting, with incredible outreach opportunities happening throughout the community. We knew immediately that we wanted to work with Pastor Muriu. We broached the idea of partnership, but Oscar held us off. Actually, he held us off for several years. He was friendly, freely sharing his insights, and asking for ours. We were blessed by being in relationship with him. But he never moved toward entering into ministry partnership with us. Finally, I pushed directly. I said, "Oscar, we are friends. You like us and we like you. Let's work together. We should be partners." Oscar was quiet for a long time before he responded, "Laurie, let me tell you about my courtship."

Pastor Oscar's story was a long one. It involved a goat, a rope, and a third party initiating conversation with the family of his future wife. He wasn't even part of the first discussions with his prospective in-laws. Slowly, through many meetings over a long period of time, the conversation between the parties wound around until the topic of marriage was broached with the family. At the end of his story, he said, "Americans are quick to jump, but you're quick to dump too. You don't understand the rest of the world. You jump in too fast without knowing enough. We move a little slower, but we keep moving in the same direction." Slowly and gently, Pastor Oscar was showing us how blind we were in understanding other cultures. We only see our own viewpoint and assume that people will want whatever we are offering. We never stop to ask what other perspectives there might be. We want to jump right in and solve problems, and in doing so, we sink the possibility of true partnership before we even begin.

As we began to realize how blind we were to the rest of the world, and to how the rest of the world saw us, our ministry was shaken. We asked over and over again, "How do we see? How do we open our eyes?" Kenton asked these questions of a dozen or more leaders from different churches and backgrounds. We took a hard look at the demographics of our staff and realized our key leadership was not very diverse. How could we encourage different perspectives if all we surrounded ourselves with were people like us?

We moved to make both our staff and elder board more diverse. We asked ourselves, "Would people from this community feel comfortable at this service? Where are we not making people feel comfortable, or like they belong?" The answers weren't always easy to hear, but we started talking less and listening more. We responded by making changes to our ministry, church services, and programs. And as a result, our congregation has become more diverse. It might take a little longer, but the outcome is beautiful.

For a real partnership to develop with the people of Minnie Street, we had to release our need to control timing and instead let the community leaders set the pace. We needed to prioritize relationships over "problem solving." We had to intentionally amplify the voices of those we were called to serve.

That does not mean that we don't also have a voice. True partnership involves mutuality. We highly value the voice, strengths, and ownership of the people in the community. Simultaneously, the church is making a significant investment of time, people, and financial resources. Remaining silent when issues arise does not build relationships. We may not agree on everything, but we do need to talk through differences of opinion that may arise. There will be bumps in any partnership, but if the relationship foundation is sound, they can be weathered together. When we focus on keeping the partnership healthy, the problems will be easier to address.

And so, we stepped back from my problem-solving-first approach and continued to meet for several more months. We worked hard to build relationships and to understand each other's viewpoints as equal partners. When we finally opened the Minnie Street Learning Center, things were more chaotic than we would have liked. Our plans for curricula, staffing, policies, and procedures all lacked the level of organization I would have preferred. It was far from perfect from my perspective, but it was just right from theirs. The big win was that we had preserved the relationships we were building. We had been accepted into the community as partners, while simultaneously the community retained a sense of healthy ownership.

The difference our approach made to the community became apparent in the sharp contrast between the learning center we had built together and one that another organization opened not long before ours in a nearby neighborhood. The other group had done all the right things from a business perspective. They'd created a beautiful space and designed research-based curricula. They opened their doors, but nobody came. They could not figure out how to get the kids in the door, while our learning center was bursting at the seams from opening day. It was the genuine mutual respect and relationship-based partnership that had made all the difference. Twenty-five years later, that is still true.

Moving into Immigration Ministry

The immigration ministry at Mariners started very quietly. Our relationship with the families of Minnie Street brought into sharp focus for us the issues immigrants were facing right in our own community. Hardworking people were being denied fair wages, medical care, and access to higher education because of their immigration status. Providing for their families left little extra to hire lawyers.

One of our members, a paralegal, decided to offer her assistance through a Saturday morning clinic. She helped people process their paperwork and guided them through the immigration system. Her clinics were a hit, and they filled an important need for two years. But when she innocently mentioned it to her law firm, they became worried that the advice she was giving might constitute liability for them. She was forced to stop.

We were periodically able to offer clinics and workshops after that, but it was never at the forefront of our ministry efforts. In those years, people from Minnie Street were not asking for immigration assistance. Our country wasn't deporting people then. Poverty was by far the bigger issue. If only we'd had more foresight and been able to predict the future crisis, perhaps we would have been better prepared when it hit.

The first big needs arose with the "Dreamers." These young people had been brought to America as children. Many spoke only English, and some didn't even realize they were "illegal." We had been educating these children in the learning center for years, and now they were ready to apply for college, only to find out that financial aid and tuition were both out of reach because they had no social security numbers. They were considered undocumented aliens in the only country they had ever known.

We started to offer legal assistance to more families. These were people with whom we had relationships. Araceli (a pseudonym) was a Dreamer who had participated in Minnie Street tutoring through her elementary and high school years. A high-achieving student, she was accepted to study at a local university. We were able to find donors to cover the cost of both her bachelor's and master's degrees. She is highly qualified, and she cannot work because her immigration status is in limbo. She cannot contribute to the society in which she has been raised. She's caught in an awful place between her personal identity and our nation's crisis with its own identity as a country of immigrants. Because we know Araceli, we have the benefit of seeing immigration not as a political debate but as a human issue affecting people we care about.

Around this time, as we were growing in our services to immigrants, we were invited to participate in a one-day workshop with the Evangelical Immigration Table in Chicago. All the biggest church leaders working on immigration were there. We were confronted with the fact that immigration was a flash point that was beginning to tear apart our country. We knew we needed to become more proactive and less reactive in our response. We invited Matt Soerens, an author of *Welcoming the Stranger: Justice, Compassion, and Truth in the Immigration Debate,* to speak at Mariners so our leaders could learn more about immigration issues.

Serving the Aliens—and Alienating the Church?

Soerens came during our annual Outreach Weekend, which is dedicated to both local and global outreach efforts of the church. It is one of the primary ways we collect funds and recruit volunteers for all outreach activities. It gives the church an opportunity to hear about ways they can join Christ in reaching the world through service.

Though our spirits (at least those of us who had been working with the kids on Minnie Street) had been stirred by the plight of the immigrant, we were unsure how the church would respond. So, for that Outreach Weekend we talked all around immigration without directly identifying it as a key issue. We chose verses that addressed God's heart for the "other," including the Good Samaritan story. When I spoke, I told the church how I had grown up believing that if I worked hard and had an education, I could make it in America, and so could anyone else. I shared how my experiences were telling me that just wasn't true. My naïve belief was my privilege talking. The kids we had invested so much in were working hard and getting their education, yet doors were slammed in their faces. I just shared what God had been showing me about my own blindness.

We didn't even have Soerens speak to the congregation as a whole. Instead, he participated in a panel meeting after services for anyone interested in learning more about immigration. It was just a blurb of an announcement among all the other volunteer opportunities presented to the church that weekend.

Yet, about 400 people of our 25,000-member congregation decided to leave the church the following week. The people who left had not even attended the immigration panel! There had been nothing partisan or antagonistic shared at the service or after. There were no arguments or even interactions. They just . . . left. Those who talked to us later said the church was becoming "too political." Serving cute, poor children was one thing, but being proactive about immigration issues was too distressing. Compassion is always a safe topic; justice is challenging.

Believing that God is the God of all races, cultures, and nationalities, we have sought to bring very diverse groups of people closer together, knowing that it makes everybody uncomfortable. The dance becomes to disrupt without destroying. To make righteously uncomfortable without driving people away. Serving in the community has made us a much more justice-minded church. Over the last twenty years, we have gone from a predominantly Caucasian upper-middle-class church to one that is very mixed racially, culturally, politically, and economically. The challenge is to continue to move toward a church that seeks the justice God describes in Isaiah 58:

> "Is not this the kind of fasting I have chosen:
> to loose the chains of injustice
>   and untie the cords of the yoke,
> to set the oppressed free
>   and break every yoke?
> Is it not to share your food with the hungry
>   and to provide the poor wanderer with shelter—
> when you see the naked, to clothe them,
>   and not to turn away from your own flesh and blood?
> Then your light will break forth like the dawn,
>   and your healing will quickly appear;
> then your righteousness will go before you,
>   and the glory of the LORD will be your rear guard.
> Then you will call, and the LORD will answer;
>   you will cry for help, and he will say: Here am I."
>
> (vv. 6–9 NIV)

It can get messy, and toes will get stepped on, but the call to seek justice is clear. This is not as simple as it sounds. Modern-day justice issues in America are not often clean. Is it a justice issue that kids who have grown up in this country, and know no other, deserve citizenship? It's definitely a wisdom and compassion issue. But is it a justice issue? This is where it becomes difficult to call the church to action. Sometimes the laws of the land and the call to "set the oppressed free" appear to be at odds with one another.

While hearts are stirred to serve the children of Minnie Street, who are so desperately in need, those same hearts may become hardened when it comes time to open places at a public university to those same children. Do we owe them an education? A job? As a nation, we have done a lot of despicable things to the people we have brought into this country to fulfill our labor needs, but not all of them are clear right-or-wrong justice issues. Regardless of our views on the broader social issues, these are definitely oppressed people. And the Bible tells me that it is my job, and the job of the church, to serve them. It is the Bible that must remain the focus.

So we keep pushing forward. Not as quickly as I want. I would not consider Mariners a leader in immigration ministry. But the church has changed in its perspectives, and that is worth celebrating. Preserving the unity of the body while still speaking truth into the lives of our members is a constant tension. One week I received a letter exhorting the church to do more for immigrants. The following week I got a letter from someone saying we are too outspoken.

Just one year after that Outreach Weekend where four hundred members left Mariners, we were listed as one of the fifteen fastest-growing congregations in the nation. The staff is diverse, with key ministry positions held by immigrants from around the world. As we have devoted ourselves to service, our church has gained an understanding that we are not insular or isolated. We are part of a global community.

Mutuality: Servant and Served

In the years since our first stumbling steps into partnership with the people of Minnie Street, we have learned and grown together. One surprising outcome was that once the learning center successfully opened, other social agencies and faith-based groups began moving into the area. The people of the community have more resources than before. The population has changed somewhat. Cambodian refugees have moved to another neighborhood. The people we serve at the original location are almost entirely from Mexico and other Spanish-speaking countries. The center continues to grow and flourish to meet the needs of the people.

We knew we were reaching closer to our desire for mutuality when the people of Minnie Street said they wanted to do something for Mariners Church. They wanted to invite us into their homes. The invitation was open to any who wanted to come to dinner. This was no token offering. To feed a small group of people a traditional Mexican meal took not only days of cooking but also a significant portion of a family's food budget. The people were adamant. They wanted us to come. By this point, we had a clear understanding that success is when we can worship and serve side by side, each recognizing that our worth and significance is found in Christ. While our initial reaction might have been to bow out of taking from families who had so little, our growing in relationship had taught us that rejecting the invitation would be insulting. Accepting would be honoring. So, we accepted.

On the night of the dinner, Mariners families and Minnie Street families met at the community center. We shared a prayer and shy smiles. Then we broke into smaller groups and headed into the apartment homes of the community. I wasn't sure what to expect. I knew that some of these people lived two families to a tiny one-bedroom apartment. Kids often slept in a hodgepodge of blankets and pillows on the living room floor. What would I see when they opened the door? The first thing I noticed was that the family had displayed the certificates and report cards of the children on a shelf immediately inside the door. The family was proud to show off these accomplishments, and they were front and center. With space at a premium, honoring the achievements of the children was the family's priority. I should have known.

Dinner was a lively affair. I happened to catch a glimpse inside the dish cupboards. They were bare. Every available dish, serving bowl, glass, cup, and utensil had been put to use for us to share the meal together. Nothing matched, and it was perfect. We talked and laughed, sometimes at each other, and sometimes at ourselves. Though we offered, we were not allowed to lift a finger. The family we visited wanted to serve us. Don't miss that: they wanted to serve us. And we were humbled.

The us-and-them paradigm is flipped on its head when the people we serve become the servants. When we recognize that we are serving each other, true mutuality is achieved, and God is honored. It doesn't have to be a tangible service, like the meal we shared. The people of Minnie Street serve us every day through generously sharing their community expertise and their cultural knowledge, and by gently challenging our own unexamined assumptions and arrogance.

We have learned so much through our twenty-plus-year relationship with our neighbors. Mariners has now created five community centers in different areas of need around us. Each center reflects the people, needs, culture, and desires of the neighborhood where it is located. The people of Minnie Street are proud to be the role models.

The journey Mariners has taken from "ministry to" to "ministry with" immigrants in our community illustrates some of the movement from hospitality to solidarity to mutuality, which is taken up in the next chapter. We at Mariners are not a perfect example of anything, but we are following Jesus where he leads, and it has been an amazing adventure.

Jeremiah 22:16 says,

> He judged the cause of the poor and needy;
>   then it was well.
> Is not this to know me?
>   says the LORD.

The Bible tells us that serving the poor, the marginalized, and those in need is vital to our health as Christians and as a congregation. God has shown us through our ongoing development in outreach that we truly do need the poor more than they need us.

～ ONE PERSON'S STORY ～

It started as a simple serving opportunity—helping a refugee family with lots of kids get settled here in America. It was a two-month commitment, tops (our personal boundaries were firm!).

All went as expected. Until the two months were up. We hadn't planned on falling in love with this family, especially the bright, beautiful, boundary-pushing kids. But we had. From that moment forward, a serving story became a love story.

Within months, one family grew to be several, and then several more, as more were settled in the same town. More beautiful, boundary-pushing kids!

A small army of folk had joined along the way—helping in any way needed. People were on call to run to the store for more diapers, more soap, and more bananas (one of a few foods that felt familiar to the newly arriving families). Others rallied to bring mountains of warm jackets, hats, and boots in every imaginable size. Winter was setting in. Groups stepped up to take kids to the park or organize a game of kickball. Anything to burn off some of that kid energy!

Before long, the army fell in love, too. Six months in, together we and the families crafted a program that would help the kids learn English, cope with school, settle into the culture. These families' culture, social status, and religion were entirely different from ours. That didn't matter. We were simply called to love. To provide a safe place. Welcoming arms. Eyes that lit up when each child entered the room. Our job was to reflect Christ's light.

More than a decade has passed. The kids are now young adults. During those years, we have done life together. All of it. Every game-winning soccer goal. Every "I'm going to prom!" celebration. Heart-heavy medical journeys. "I had a car accident!" urgent phone calls. "I just got accepted to college!" jubilation. And it wasn't a one-way thing. When my husband had a serious medical event, the moment the word got out, his phone blew up with calls from all of his "boys"—profoundly concerned. (We had to stop them from flooding the hospital all at once!) We have done deaths. We have done births. We have done the highest of highs and lowest of lows. We have done life. In their words, and ours, we are family.

Frankly—and maybe oddly—it's hard for us to think of "doing evangelism" when it comes to family.

Think about it in terms of your own family. How often do you ponder how to "evangelize" your son or your daughter? My guess is, you don't think about it in those terms. It seems awkward . . . dare I say, a little weird? You love that child with your entire being. You would take a bullet for your son. You passionately desire your daughter's well-being and would do anything you could to further it. In that context, you deeply desire for your son to know and fully embrace Jesus Christ, the Rescuer. That's how we feel about our refugee kids, too. It's never really been about "doing evangelism."

Now that they are young adults, it is not unusual to have a deep, rich conversation about loads of things—including matters of faith. Theirs and ours. There is authentic, mutual respect. There is active listening. There is a desire to learn and understand—and we have learned much from them! When the Holy Spirit opens the door, we do our best to walk through it. We have to fight the urge to overtalk, to overpresent. Instead, we try to listen to his promptings, literally asking, "What do you want us to say in this moment?" Then the next. Then the next. We avoid the peripheral. The debates and arguments. At least for now, we stick to the core question, as we see it, for their lives (and, frankly, ours as well): Who is Jesus really?

I can only say, many of those conversations have felt deeply anointed.

At the end of the day, we know we must "stay in our own lane." If the Spirit doesn't open the door, we never force it. Our job is to love and reflect Jesus as best we can . . . and articulate his rescuing grace when the door opens. We pray passionately and unceasingly, as you do for your own kids . . . come, Lord Jesus, come. Do what only you can do.

May it be so.

—*A grateful Christ follower and World Relief volunteer*

4

BEYOND WELCOMING

Sandra Maria van Opstal

Bienvenido. Bienvenue. Aloha. You've seen those posters with the dozens of ways you can say welcome. "Welcome" is a word used to communicate "there is room for you." In Chipewyan (an indigenous language from northern Canada), that's what the literal translation is. Here is what is engraved on our symbol of welcome, the Statue of Liberty, also known as the mother of exiles:

> Give me your tired, your poor
> Your huddled masses yearning to breathe free
> The wretched refuse of your teeming shore
> Send these, the homeless, tempest-tossed to me
> I lift my lamp beside the golden door!

"You're more than welcome": it's a phrase most of us use regularly. Whether we're being thanked for a service, or sharing our home or our table with others, these words get used on a regular basis in various contexts. But truthfully, we don't fully understand what they mean. Like so many other well-worn phrases in our common language, we say it without thinking of its implications or deeper meaning.

Another phrase we hear regularly, especially in our churches, is "welcoming the stranger." Maybe we have a hospitality team or a team of greeters at church; maybe our kids are talking about it in Sunday school, or there's a reference to it in conversations—but again, many of us are not pausing to discern the implicit call we have to go beyond an action or task to a shift in our state of being or identity.

What is this shift, this journey from doing to being? It involves a deepening relationship with both the Holy Spirit and people who may not look like us or share our experiences. Shifting our focus from doing to being allows us to become more fully the community that Scripture calls us to be. Though we may begin with hospitality, where we are saying "we welcome you," Scripture calls us to journey from that place, through a place of solidarity ("we stand with you"), and ultimately to mutuality ("we need you"), where we comprehend just how deeply the global community of Jesus followers *need* each other in order to be the people of God we are called by Scripture to be.

In his letter to the Philippians, Paul expresses this in the concept of "oneness": "If then there is any encouragement in Christ, any consolation from love, any sharing in the Spirit, any compassion and sympathy, make my joy complete: be of the same mind, having the same love, being in full accord and of one mind" (Phil. 2:1–2). If oneness is the goal, the outcome, the result, then what is the activity that leads to the result? Paul goes on to make this clear: "Do nothing from selfish ambition or conceit, but in humility regard others as better than yourselves. Let each of you look not to your own interests, but to the interests of others" (vv. 3–4). So, what does it mean to take this journey? To follow a path that we've likely never walked before? First, we must understand what true hospitality is.

Esperanza (not her real name) arrived at the Mexico/US border in 2014, seven months pregnant, holding her toddler by the hand, having endured a painful and dangerous journey from Central America. She was escaping a life-threatening situation, hoping for safety in the United States, and she ultimately ended up in our community on the west side of Chicago. As my family got to know her, our kids became friends, and so did we—sharing child care, walks to the park, and court dates as we fought alongside her for the asylum paperwork and services she desperately needed. Esperanza had keys to and an open invitation to my home, and I regularly stopped by to check in or to have her watch my son. I wanted her to know that although she might feel unwelcomed because of her experiences in our country, she belonged to our community and there was room for her. Hospitality was not convenient for me, my family, or our church. In the case of Esperanza, it was uncomfortable and at times costly. Welcome isn't just a word we speak but a way we live. And we live this welcome in a countercultural way that distinguishes us as people who follow a God of compassion and love. Esperanza was a Christian, but many of her friends who were also immigrant parents were not, although they had grown up with spiritual roots. Imagine what her friends in the community experienced about the church to which she belonged and the way they welcomed her in and stood by her. What testimony was "spoken" by the actions of hospitality, and the words that accompanied those actions?

The Call to Hospitality

We are all at least partially familiar with our biblical call to hospitality: from Jesus's exhortation to "love our neighbor" and his discussion with the rich man about who his neighbor is (Mark 10:17–31; Luke 10:25–37), to the early church in Acts 2, where they "devoted themselves" to it. "Welcoming the stranger" is another phrase we often hear, specifically when discussing immigrants, refugees, or people we don't know or who might not fit into our familiar context. This phrase is rooted in Exodus 19 and Matthew 25. In the latter, Jesus clarifies who will enter the kingdom of God:

> "Then the king will say to those at his right hand, 'Come, you that are blessed by my Father, inherit the kingdom prepared for you from the foundation of the world; for I was hungry and you gave me food, I was thirsty and you gave me something to drink, **I was a stranger and you welcomed me**, I was naked and you gave me clothing, I was sick and you took care of me, I was in prison and you visited me.' Then the righteous will answer him, 'Lord, when was it that we saw

you hungry and gave you food, or thirsty and gave you something to drink? And when was it that we saw you a stranger and welcomed you, or naked and gave you clothing? And when was it that we saw you sick or in prison and visited you?' And the king will answer them, 'Truly I tell you, just as you did it to one of the least of these who are members of my family, you did to me.'" (vv. 34–40)

Interestingly, this teaching of Jesus comes right after the parable of the ten virgins (who were not ready when the king showed up) and the parable of the wicked servant (who didn't really understand the values in which the master operates). Here again, we see people who are in front of Jesus who do not understand the nature of the king or his kingdom. Let's not be too hard on them. As Christians, we often need mentors, friends, and the Holy Spirit's work in our lives to deepen our revelation.

This hospitality narrative is a vital step in our process of living out Christ's command to be the church and to show compassion and mercy to those who need it most (Eph. 4:32; Phil. 2:1). However, it is only a first step. Though there is a level of comfort for the church with hospitality, and a temptation to pat ourselves on the back because we have been so welcoming, we will miss out on the gifts our global family have to offer if we stop there. If we never move past the idea of hospitality as a task to be accomplished, we remain stuck in a limited paradigm. A power structure is involved here, as well: if we're only focused on providing hospitality, especially to immigrants and refugees, then the church stays in a position of power. We retain the comfort level that any majority culture enjoys: no one is asking much of us, and we take few risks in this process.

We also must remember that true hospitality goes deeper than the initial words of welcome; what matters is how we practice welcome. Oscar left Acapulco when he was sixteen, with his ten- and twelve-year-old brothers and his mother, to reunite with his father. After they crossed the border, the coyote shouted "*la migra*" (ICE) and scrambled off, leaving them in the desert without anything. They walked for about a day and stumbled into someone's yard. The family had the means to take them in and provide housing, food, clothes, communication with their family, and bus tickets for their journey. Given the situation and the language barrier, this Christian family did not overtly evangelize them with words; instead, they "overtly loved" them. They were the sole reason this mother and three boys were able to survive the desert and find their way home to Chicago. This older white Christian couple did not share very much in common with them socially; however, they knew they were called to love. When the migrant family asked how they could pay them back, for example, by sending money, the Christian couple told them it would be enough for them to find a church when they reached Chicago. While they had been in a religious context in the broader Latin American culture, they were not Christians.

When the immigrant family arrived in their new city, they connected with an immigrant church, where they encountered God through the preaching of the Word, the experience of worship, and the witness of this church that caused a spiritual awakening. Their very first day in Chicago was a Sunday. The parents went to work selling tamales and sent the boys to church. They had been told of the hospitality of this particular neighborhood church. This local church works with returning citizens, as well as engaging in the parole process; in other words, the church building is much more than a place for congregants to come and meet God. On any given day, someone may enter the church building with a particular tangible need, but by doing so, the person engages with pastors and leaders who are embodying the grace, mercy, and love of Christ in how they meet those needs.

This story shows hospitality in two forms: a nonimmigrant family offering to share their home with a migrant family, and an immigrant church receiving the migrant family and witnessing to them. It was both the "overt love" of an older white Christian couple and the "welcome" of an immigrant church that allowed them to live. They were revived spiritually, and they have made an incredible life for themselves as entrepreneurs. You will still find these men selling tamales on Pulaski and cutting hair on Kedzie when they are not serving at church in Little Village.

Imagine that your intent is to be a good neighbor to immigrants in your community: as a result, you perpetually invite them over. They come into your home, where you serve them food of your choice, play music (or not) of your choice, have them sit at a table or in chairs of your choice. In this setting, you have the power as the host. Maybe we've not thought about it that way before, but it is true. "Welcoming into" allows the one welcoming to preserve the power in the relationship while feeling as though he or she is doing something fantastic. Imagine an immigrant family who has been coming to your church for food, clothing, kids' programs, or other services. You begin a relationship with them in which they are clearly the ones "in need." You have a genuine desire to care for the hungry, hurting, and lost, and to show the Lord's compassion. Yes, we should applaud that countercultural act in such a narcissistic season of Christian faith. That is a step that is desired for every Christian. The problem is that if your relationships are one-directional, the people you are helping will not engage freely. They may allow you to pray for them, they may attend your Bible studies, but you may never know if their "curiosity" for Jesus is authentic or an act of obligation.

Consider some perspective applied from the Cultural Intelligence Center, an organization that studies interaction among people from diverse backgrounds. People who come from non-Western contexts have a high value for preserving harmony, so they are not likely to directly decline an invitation. Many also come from contexts that have a high-power distance, which means that if you have more age, credentials, or authority, or are a white American, they are likely to recognize the power in the relationship and operate out of deference. Most white Americans, due to our deeply understood egalitarian values and direct communication, would miss the cues that we might be backing people into a proverbial corner without intending or knowing we are doing so. A family in our community experienced some housing scarcity and moved in with one of our congregants. They did not come from a faith background, and no one "forced" them to join any church activities, but, given their Latin American culture, they did not feel they could decline the invitations. They did not say no, but they often had a conflict with the time of the events. They often came and never directly declined. When they moved out of the apartment into their own space a few blocks away, they skipped most events and attended only back-to-school fairs or community-wide events. Did they genuinely have interest in knowing Jesus, or did they feel pressure from the church leader, given their positive view of hierarchy, or were they merely saving face with their attendance? We will never know the answer.

Standing in Solidarity

So, if deepening our understanding of true hospitality and opening our hearts to it are the first step, what's next? How do we as a church continue to engage in our biblical calling as expressed in Ephesians 2:11–22 to both hospitality and solidarity?

In this passage, Paul reminds the Ephesians that they were once aliens and strangers who had no hope. This word choice is not a mistake; he's reminding them that they were once outcast and considered "less than" by God's chosen people, in much the same way immigrants and refugees are treated in our country (especially in this current atmosphere). They are told they are aliens—dangerous intruders who can't stand on their own feet. Beyond anti-immigrant rhetoric, our nation's policies and processes remind immigrants and refugees that they are barely human. This includes all groups that fall under this title: those who are undocumented, those who seek asylum, and even those who are here legally but require some financial assistance due to family hardship. Imagine feeling like everything about you is unacceptable, whether you are poor, educated professionals, or just children. But now there's hope! Those who "once were far off have been brought near by the blood of Christ," and he "has made both groups into one and has broken down the dividing wall, that is, the hostility between us" (vv. 13b, 14b). In other words, they are to stand with each other, to view each other as equals, as family in the body of Christ. When we stand with Oscar by welcoming him into our congregation or with Esperanza by neighboring her, Oscar and Esperanza experience tangibly the reality Paul outlines to the church in Ephesus. Unity moves from being a concept to the lived theology embodied by daily and even mundane actions. This is also a step in our journey toward loving the immigrants and refugees who come to our country, city, and community, toward understanding that every person bears God's image and has equal access to the kingdom. The gospel is available to all, transforms all, and invites all to equal participation in God's family. This countercultural solidarity was the power of the gospel in Paul's time, and still is today.

Solidarity is not sharing a building. I could tell you countless stories of white evangelical communities who have sought to be in solidarity with immigrant communities. It usually plays out one of two ways. The first is the "client" relationship, which is based in services and help to a financially underresourced community that are transactional. This relationship of compassion creates a distinctive power dynamic where there is a benevolent "giver" and an indebted "receiver." The second is the "tenant" relationship, which is based in shared space. The immigrant community is renting or using space in a building. This relationship does not usually result in connectedness because the immigrant community does not feel obliged to participate in activities with their landlords. Immigrants, particularly the most vulnerable, are looking for people who will stand *with* them—not *for* them. They are inviting us to come and stand alongside them.

Imagine a third way where the focus is not on delivering or sharing assets but on relating as neighbors in proximity to one another. Rejoicing when one rejoices and suffering when one suffers (Rom. 12:15). I can almost taste the gluten and butter, and look forward to dropping them off. Communities that neighbor well become a fragrant offering; they draw people to authentic relationship with the community and with Jesus. We become the doors that people knock on because they smell us down the street.

Mari and Diego came to the door because they had heard there were showers in the building. They had been sleeping in the streets with their children because they did not feel safe accessing shelter/housing due to a lack of privacy for their girls. They came into the church to shower and found brothers and sisters who would listen, learn, and lean in to their story. They found a family that would offer hospitality by welcoming them in and embody solidarity by standing with them in practical ways. They not only had their physical needs met, they found a community to which they could belong.

Carlos and Sara rang the buzzer at our church looking for someone to help them with their marriage. They were not congregants, and they were not clients of the community center. They were simply people who smelled the fragrance of a community that stood in solidarity with people by being present with them in tangible ways. They wanted to meet face-to-face with someone who could help them be on a road to recovery in their marriage.

In all these cases the first contact with the church communities was not spiritual curiosity but emotional or physical needs. And these churches did not turn them away or attempt to tell them what they needed; they leaned in. They embodied love beyond hospitality, which welcomes you into solidarity, which is the act of being with people in all their joy and needs.

So, why is solidarity important? Standing in solidarity in the form of relationship, relief, and advocacy witnesses to the gospel. It is a witness not only to immigrants but also to those who are not followers of Jesus whose experience of evangelical Christians is that we are xenophobic. If nonimmigrant churches and immigrant churches work together to address the suffering of immigrants and the broken aspects of our immigration system that separates children from families, this becomes a witness to all who see the relationship of solidarity.

Witness the Christian leaders in the migrant caravan of over eight thousand Central Americans, who are working with Mexican pastors and Latinx churches in Southern California through the Matthew 25 So-Cal ministry. They're doing so in partnership with white nonimmigrant churches who historically have not done anything to impact our immigration policies through bipartisan reform but are now beginning to enter this process. This is a reciprocal partnership of four different entities standing together in the name of Jesus and standing for the importance of the family unit. Central Americans, Mexicans, Latinx, and nonimmigrant white communities are working together to model that the power of the gospel is indeed potent. This entire group is becoming a powerful witness of Christ's love to nonbelieving immigrants and to church-adjacent people in the United States who are watching the statistics on white evangelicals.

To truly enter this stage of solidarity in our relationships, we as the church need to be engaging our brothers and sisters with questions:

- What issues most impact you?
- What do you need?
- How can we stand with you?
- What can we celebrate with you?

These are questions we should be asking consistently, both as a church community and as individuals. It is the privilege of any majority culture to assume that we know or understand the needs of other cultures and the issues that most impact them, and that we are the ones best equipped to address those issues. But to make this assumption misses the point; we cannot truly stand in solidarity with this perspective. We must move ourselves from a position of power and privilege to a place where we are standing next to a stranger who is becoming a friend. To speak the truth of God's character into the lives of displaced people, we must earn their respect and trust from a position of learning and humility.

True solidarity grows out of real empathy for what another individual or group are experiencing, and how they are impacted by systemic issues that are deeply embedded in our national psyche. To grow this empathy, we need to be "doing life with" immigrants, experiencing what they experience, sharing meals, attending immigration appointments with a family, advocating for resources, and otherwise communicating that "you matter to us." Working toward solidarity helps to minimize the power dynamic that has been too often prevalent in our approach to displaced communities, which can be damaging to the very people we're trying to help; it says, "we need you as part of our community," "please help us understand your struggles, your challenges, and all the things you have to offer."

When churches focus on solidarity, they are exhibiting an additional level of cultural competence, which is often not present where hospitality is the primary focus. However, even solidarity allows us who are citizens to retain power, because we perceive that they need us but we do not need them. We are showing a desire to understand others' perspective and needs but can miss important elements of God's call to us to live in reciprocity as a global church. There's a vital next step in the process that moves us more fully into connectedness. And as immigration advocate Karen González says, "Welcoming AND belonging are overarching narratives of the Bible."

Powerful moments happen when nonimmigrant, Latinx, and immigrant Christians come together to pray, act, and speak out in one united voice. I have had more conversations about my faith at the border, in the halls of our nation's capital, or during protests on the streets of my city than in any church-sanctioned gatherings. The conversations with Latinx community leaders who are spiritually interested but skeptical of the church have been profound. This is especially true on topics of justice, where the church has been silent and is now speaking up.

The Stage of Mutuality

This next stage of the journey is mutuality. Mutuality was at the core of the early church's witness in the world. The testimony of the church in Acts 4:31–37 centers around how they lived in mutuality. Note what is said about them upon receiving the power of the Spirit.

> When they had prayed, the place in which they were gathered was shaken; and they were all filled with the Holy Spirit and spoke the word of God with boldness. Now the whole group of those who believed were of one heart and soul, and no one claimed private ownership of any possessions, but everything they owned was held in common. With great power the apostles gave their testimony to the resurrection of the Lord Jesus, and great grace was upon them all. There was not a needy person among them, for as many as owned

lands or houses sold them and brought the proceeds of what was sold. They laid it at the apostles' feet, and it was distributed to each as any had need. (vv. 31–35)

Note that the passage does not start by saying that the powerful and wealthy shared. It says that "no one" claimed any of their possessions as their own. This means that everyone brought what they had to the community. Did some have more material possessions than others? Of course. That is true today—some of us make four times what others of us do, often in the same congregation. What can't be missed here is that they *all* shared. The Spirit empowered them, they developed relationship and were unified, and they shared everything. From this lifestyle and practice of mutuality they witnessed and testified to the power of the gospel. God's power was at work in them to live in a way where there were not givers and receivers but brothers and sisters.

In a majority culture primarily focused on individualism, we are often blind to our deep need for this in our own relationships, let alone in our churches and communities. As a result, we may miss what is sometimes called "cultural competence plus": living out the idea that we need each other in the body of Christ.

Our church communities in the United States (especially those that are primarily white) are used to operating from the perspective that most church communities approach church life as we do. In reality, we have just as much (if not more) to learn and receive from global Christians as we have to teach and give. However, to truly enter into a space of mutuality, we must ask more of ourselves than we are accustomed to.

Mutuality involves vulnerability and dependence, acknowledging that we don't "have it all together," that we need each other, and that we have much to learn and many places where we need to grow. Imagine a place where this is lived out across cultures and socioeconomic power! To truly live out mutuality, we must remove ourselves from a position of power and acknowledge the fears and hesitancy of change in how we operate.

Karen González captures the biblical nuance of hospitality and solidarity that leads to mutuality: "Ultimately, as the church, we are called to mutuality—to a perspective that says 'We need each other.' Again, there is a power dynamic that is often missed in our current approach to hospitality and even solidarity, whose subtext is 'you need us,' 'we're here to help,' and 'how can we fix this for you?'"[1] Whether we consciously think this way or not, we perpetuate that power dynamic by approaching our ministry to immigrants in this way.

What's an example of mutuality starting to happen in ministry? How do we move into a new perspective and begin to implement mutuality in our ministry? It may be simpler than you think: Romans 12:15 calls us to rejoice with those who rejoice, and mourn with those who mourn. In Luke 14, Jesus tells two parables of great banquets where the guests came from unexpected places. One example of how these things can come together is in the way that we worship. Western worship styles generally don't allow space for lament; our songs and traditions tend to leave out this aspect. However, other cultures practice this discipline regularly. So, how can we, in our Western, American churches, incorporate this practice and learn from those who do practice it?

One example is how we approach songs of worship. When planning songs of lament as part of a worship service, do we think, "We should sing this because Ananya and Sam (who come from cultures where lament is commonly a part of worship) are here today"? Or do we think, "How can we learn from this practice and allow Ananya and Sam to teach us what they've learned from Scripture about lament and how they incorporate biblical lament into worship?"

Ultimately, mutuality has a lot to do with awareness, and even cultural and emotional intelligence. When I come into a relational situation (a church service, a small group, a social gathering, or a meeting), am I aware of what I'm bringing to the table, whether literally or figuratively? Am I willing to embrace my need for others to teach me, to be vulnerable about the areas where I need to grow, and to do so with love?

When we are able to get to a place where we embrace strangers rather than simply welcoming them, where we see them as family members (brothers or sisters), the church as a whole and its community become a witness for Christ's love! We do this by practicing love in such a way that we communicate that "there's something to be learned from every human being." Embracing the fullness of mutuality becomes our credibility in the Word. As Jesus reminded us, "They will know you are my disciples if you *love one another*." And true love requires mutuality.

González further amplifies this through the story of Hagar by showing us that we are also in need. While we may preach the gospel and connect others to the truth of Jesus, proximity allows us to encounter the presence of Jesus.

> Hagar in the desert reminds all of us that the Spirit can be found in the places we least expect: with the poor, the outcasts, the enslaved people, the domestic help, and the foreigners. God is present with anyone who is treated as a human resource rather than a human being. God shows up not just for the master and mistress of the house and the native citizens with rights but also for the undocumented maid in the kitchen. And who would have imagined that the undocumented maid didn't just bring needs—for refuge or economic opportunity? Who knew that she also brought gifts: faith and devotion, hard work, talents, rich cultural traditions, and a family that would grow up and integrate into the adopted country?[2]

Christ's Body as Witness

Evangelism in a Western context has been seen as communicating truths. Biblical witness is about operating in a way that shows the transformative reality of Jesus. Particularly in church planting in Latino contexts, it requires a lot of face time and relationship building. Research done by the Send Institute of the Billy Graham Center at Wheaton College is showing that this method of relational process is vital in evangelism. People want to be seen, accepted, and included. This is especially true for communities that are socially marginalized. And it is amplified for groups that have experienced displacement, because they have been forced to leave their lands and feel disconnected from place and all that means.

This is hard to understand for people in the United States, for whom mobility is an expected luxury. We have an impoverished understanding of place. Imagine the impact of dislocation on people from indigenous cultures, such as those coming from Mexico and Central America, who feel deeply connected to their lands and who have had to leave to survive. Imagine the opportunity for their inclusion that we have as Jesus followers. In *Reimagining Evangelism*, Rick Richardson repeats his mantra that people want a community to belong to before they want something to believe in. Immigrants come from many different experiences, but whether they lived in poverty or not, in their relocation they desire to belong. Churches are presented with the opportunity to be "home away from home." We are provided an opportunity to embody and witness to the love of Christ. Not in what we say but in how we live (1 John).

God's gift to us is Christ's body. When we think of Christ's body, many of us think of Holy Communion or the Lord's Supper, the practice Jesus gave us not only to remember him but "in memory" of him. The practice allows us to partake in a practice to remember his many words to us about who he is and who we are. We are his body.

By inviting others to Jesus, we are inviting them to an embodied process of hospitality, solidarity, and mutuality with other members of his body. We are reminding them that when they say yes to Jesus, they are saying yes to his body as described in Romans 12:5: "so we, who are many, are one body in Christ, and individually we are members one of another." Think of the examples of reaching out to Esperanza and all the examples of verbalizing and demonstrating Christ's love discussed in this chapter.

These acts of hospitality, solidarity, and mutuality provide not only salvation for the one coming into relationship with Jesus but also an ongoing transformation and freedom for those who are in Christ. This is why we are urged by Paul to consider the importance of how this body functions together. He urges in 1 Corinthians 12:24–26: "But God has so arranged the body, giving the greater honor to the inferior member, that there may be no dissension within the body, but the members may have the same care for one another. If one member suffers, all suffer together with it; if one member is honored, all rejoice together with it."

While we tend to think of this journey from hospitality to mutuality as a one-way process, our life in Christ is far from linear. Jesus exemplified mutuality in every way: in the stories he told, in the way he related to others, and even in the way he died. When the church works to embody mutuality in their daily life, and especially in their approach to immigrants and refugees, we learn to lament, celebrate, and learn together. Ultimately, this leads to the healing and wholeness that God wants for his creation! And this means not just doing but *being* the reflection of Christ's love, which the church is called to be; to witness to Christ not just in our words but in our *mutual* identity as members of his body.

~~ ONE PERSON'S STORY ~~

On January 29, 2018, I got into an ambulance bound for Durham, North Carolina, with my five-month-old daughter, Maryam, sickly and clearly run down from all the hospital procedures she had undergone. My wife, Zakera, and our two sons followed behind with a family friend, Nasrein, for a medical journey that we hoped would be short and successful. Boarding the ambulance, I was unaware of how long we would await my daughter's results. I do not remember much from that day except the anxiety I felt of the unknown.

It all started one cold afternoon in Charlotte when I called the doctor and told him that Maryam was bleeding from her eyes and nose, and he said to take her immediately to the hospital. After her examination, the doctors immediately referred us to Duke Hospital in Durham. I did not carry anything with me besides Maryam. Upon arriving, my children slept on the hospital benches while the doctors were with my daughter.

For the whole year since arriving in the United States, my kids had a home and were safe, but Maryam's illness changed this. After a long wait marked by uncertainty, a family friend contacted the only person she knew in the area. She connected us to Gihan from Islamic Relief, who provided us with housing for two days. We lived in the hospital cafeteria by day and our temporary housing by night with several other families.

On the third day in Durham, my boys and I moved into Hope House, a shelter provided by Hope Valley Baptist Church, while Zakera and Maryam stayed at the hospital. At Hope House, we met Mr. Bill Bigger from Hope Valley Baptist Church and Allison Perry from World Relief, whom Gihan had contacted for further help. During our drive from the hospital, Allison told me that Hope House, in collaboration with Hope Valley Baptist Church, would provide us with long-term temporary housing. They recognized our vulnerability as refugees in dire need of a place to stay as our daughter continued receiving treatment.

Mr. Bill was such a good man. It was easy to see how much he cared for my family, especially when he came to play with my children. I will never forget how he broke down with me when I told him that Maryam was going through a liver transplant. After Bill passed, I attended prayers at the church. Mr. Mark, the new pastor, and other members sat with me, hugged me, and told me that the church would continue supporting me. They were all kind to me, and they have been since the death of Mr. Bill.

I am thankful for the many people who have supported my family. I love living here. My family is now safe, and we are slowly regaining what we lost during the many months of Maryam's sickness. My kids have started school, and Maryam can now access the hospital easily. This has been my experience of Christians reaching out and their way of life here.

—*Abdul Nazari*

5

PUBLIC WITNESS AND ADVOCACY

Jenny Yang

The image of Alan Kurdi, a five-year-old Syrian refugee boy, washed up on the shores of Turkey captured international attention in the summer of 2015. Wearing a red T-shirt, blue shorts, and Velcro sneakers, he had drowned trying to find safety in a country not his own. He catapulted the image of the refugee into the minds of people around the world as a little boy who could be one of our children, one of our neighbors and friends. From a narrative that focused on the millions of refugees who were "invading" and "swarming" the West, suddenly a common humanity was formed in which we now believed that the refugee crisis was not about "them" anymore but about us.

So much of the public discourse around refugees in the United States and around the world has been about national security or economics, but Alan crystallized for us the tragic human cost of little children who have no safe place to go. He also sparked a national debate about what our response should be, and people around the country starting speaking out in ways they hadn't before to support refugees. A new grassroots campaign called We Welcome Refugees was launched, for example, under the leadership of Ann Voskamp, a *New York Times* best-selling author, and Vickie Reddy, then the coleader of the Justice Conference. The campaign started a petition to press governments to welcome refugees that garnered around nineteen thousand signatures, and it became an active community that used its voice to speak out in support of refugees. Such public actions demonstrated that for many Christians, caring for refugees wasn't just about an individual interaction with them but also about creating a welcoming society where just policies and laws would lead to the flourishing of our most vulnerable neighbors.

Starting the Advocacy Journey

The importance of advocacy, or the use of our voice, became clear to me when I studied abroad in Madrid, Spain. I was taking the subway back home after class when I saw a young African woman with her child riding in the same car. A group of Spanish teenagers suddenly boarded the train and started to scrawl graffiti on the walls in Spanish: "Get out of my country black people!" I could tell that the young African woman felt uncomfortable and insecure, but before I could say anything to the teens, they abruptly left at the next stop. It bothered me that such a blatant instance of racism happened in front of me, but what bothered me even more was that no one on that train confronted the teenagers or even stood with the woman who was feeling vulnerable. I asked the woman if she was okay, but she didn't want to talk—she probably just wanted to get off the train. I started thinking that for this woman to truly feel welcome, she would need both legal protections from the government and a sense of belonging proffered by her community. If she had the legal right to live and work in Spain but continued to experience such racist incidents, she probably would not feel welcome or secure. If she had a welcoming community but no legal protections, she would also continue to feel vulnerable. That summer, I studied asylum law at the United Nations High Commissioner for Refugees (UNHCR) and also volunteered at an antiracism organization setting up events and rallies against racism in communities in Spain.

Creating welcome and inclusion at the individual, personal level is important, but laws and structures that govern society also directly impact whether a person experiences true shalom, or flourishing. The good news of Jesus is that he died for our sins, but he also came to Earth to heal, restore, and dignify those whom society marginalized, castigated, and oppressed. Jesus asked his followers to repent, but he also healed, comforted, and restored people in the process. Effective evangelism means not just speaking about who Jesus is but demonstrating the good news of the kingdom of God through our words, deeds, and actions toward our neighbors. The story of the Good Samaritan clearly indicates that the person who showed mercy to the man beaten up on the side of the road is the one who truly loved his neighbor. But Martin Luther King Jr. adds further nuance to this text in his "Letter from Birmingham Jail" by saying, "On the one hand, we are called to play the Good Samaritan on life's roadside, but that will be only an initial act. One day we must come to see that the whole Jericho Road must be transformed so that men and women will not be constantly beaten and robbed as they make their journey on life's highway. True compassion is more than flinging a coin to a beggar. It comes to see that an edifice which produces beggars needs restructuring." Our service toward those who are hurting is a way to demonstrate love of neighbor, but altering systems and structures is also critical to ensure that our neighbors thrive.

Pursuing Justice in the Public Square / Advocacy and Speaking Up

Part of pursuing justice means recognizing that sin not only perpetuates our individual lives but also embeds itself in the very structures and systems that are created by sinful human beings. Thus, individuals reside within systems and structures that are plagued with sin and brokenness that can perpetuate poverty, oppression, and injustice. Without our voice and advocacy, such systems can continue unchallenged and unchanged for decades, if not centuries. The church is called to bring the whole gospel not just to set sinful individuals free but to challenge and change sinful systems to allow for the flourishing of all. Slavery and apartheid, for example, were unjust systems that separated, enslaved, and oppressed individuals and pooled power within a select group of privileged people. Such systems lasted decades until individuals started speaking out and organizing to challenge the status quo. Our voice is thus critical to change structural systemic issues and address root causes of injustice.

Altering systems and structures is advocacy, or "seeking with, and on behalf of, the poor to address underlying causes of poverty and injustice through influencing the policies and practices of the powerful" (from TearFund, an evangelical organization in the UK). There are plenty of important ways that we should love our neighbors on an interpersonal level—that's most of the missional work we do. But when systemic injustice is at the root of a problem, loving our neighbor means advocacy as well.

God is a God of justice who advocates for the vulnerable, which include the "quartet of the vulnerable"—the poor, the widow, the orphan, and the immigrant. God acknowledged their vulnerabilities and instituted structures and systems to take care of them. In Deuteronomy, God specifically legislated rules to ensure that their needs were met. "When you reap your harvest in your field and forget a sheaf in the field, you shall not go back to get it; it shall be left for the alien, the orphan, and the widow, so that the LORD your God may bless you in all your undertakings. When you beat your olive trees, do not strip what is left; it shall be for the alien, the orphan, and the widow. When you gather the grapes of your vineyard, do not glean what is left; it shall be for the alien, the orphan, and the widow" (Deut. 24:19–21). Throughout Scripture, whenever such systems and structures broke down, God used the prophets to highlight the ongoing need to protect vulnerable individuals (Isa. 5:8; Mal. 3:5; Zech. 7:10).

These prophets reflected God to the world, as God acted out of his own character to pursue justice in the world. For example, "He *defends* the cause of the fatherless and the widow, and loves the foreigner residing among you, giving them food and clothing" (Deut. 10:18 NIV); "The LORD *watches over the foreigner* and sustains the fatherless and the widow" (Ps. 146:9 NIV); "Do *not oppress* the widow or the fatherless, the foreigner or the poor" (Zech. 7:10 NIV); "I will be quick to *testify against* . . . those who defraud laborers of their wages, who oppress the widows and the fatherless, and deprive the foreigners among you . . . of justice" (Mal. 3:5 NIV).

For us as bearers of God's image in the world, we must also do the very things God does in Scripture—defend, watch over, not oppress, and testify against injustice in the world as a way to pursue justice and love our neighbor. As followers of Christ, we cannot truly love our neighbor without engaging the structures and systems in which our neighbors live. Unless certain policies and practices change, the situation of poor and marginalized people around the world is unlikely to improve over the long term. Clive Calver, the president of World Relief, once said, "You cannot effectively share the gospel with a hungry child without also giving that child something to eat." Effective evangelism is sharing the good news of Jesus and also seeking the restoration of what is broken in our society.

Challenging the Dominant Narrative on Refugees

There is a common, dominant narrative about refugees that says they're a burden, unwelcome, and perhaps to blame for their own woes. It has led to the shutting of doors, to a lack of empathy, to hardening, and to more restrictive migration policies that have led to dire, even deadly, consequences for refugees. Refugees have taken more perilous routes to cross borders, oceans, and lands to seek safety. In the summer of 2015, for example, when refugees became mistakenly linked to the terrorist bombings in Paris, thirty-one US state governors declared that they did not want Syrian refugees resettled to their states.[1] And we in the US church, instead of seeing the humanity of refugees and having refugee stories impact the way we see and understand God, have often closed our hearts and minds to seeing how we could help, protect, and assist the very people God tells us to care for.

From Genesis to Revelation, the Bible is a story about migration, of people moving from one place to another—from Abraham, who was called to leave his homeland and migrate elsewhere; to Ruth, a Moabite migrant worker gleaning the fields, whose hard work ethic caught the attention of Boaz; to Paul in the New Testament, who was persecuted and migrated to new areas to share the gospel. God's heart toward migrants is to show compassion and mercy to them, as he exhorted the Israelites repeatedly to treat the migrant "as your native born" (Lev. 19:34 NIV). This was a reminder to the Israelite people that they were migrants themselves, and they were to be particularly concerned for those who were vulnerable, including migrants, orphans, and widows.

For many Christians, however, immigration is completely separate from their biblical worldview. They see immigration as a political issue, not as a biblical issue. A LifeWay Research poll carried out in 2015 found that the media (at 16 percent) influenced evangelical thinking on immigration more than did the Bible (12 percent) or the local church (2 percent).[2] Many of us are aware, especially in our social media interactions, that conversations around immigration don't refer to biblical teachings necessarily but consist of economics, politics, and national security arguments. These factors should be a part of the conversation, but they shouldn't be the only factors in it. How Jesus would want us to respond, both at a personal and at a structural level, is critically important in forming our response as Christians distinctive from the world's response.

This lack of a biblical worldview on migration has led to many Christians fearing refugees. A different LifeWay Research poll found that churches were more likely (44 percent) to fear refugees than to help them locally (9 percent).[3] This fear is not rooted in the reality that refugees are harmful to national security; the Cato Institute, a libertarian think tank in Washington, DC, found that the likelihood of someone dying in a terrorist attack by refugees was 1 in 3.6 billion. But rather, this fear is due to misinformation about who refugees are and perhaps the demographic and cultural changes that will happen due to refugees coming into local communities.

In fact, the same survey found that most churches have not done anything to respond to the global refugee crisis. At a time of intense humanitarian crises around the world, instead of welcoming the vulnerable, persecuted, and oppressed and calling for compassionate policies to protect them, we have felt more comfortable with building walls and insulating ourselves from feeling the pain of others. Compounding this lack of compassion is discomfort with having new neighbors who may be of a different religion or nationality. Refugees are often considered a terrorist threat, a nuisance, or a threat to Christianity.

The discipleship we offer through the local church is the foundation we need to form a biblical worldview, and teaching the biblical story of migration and biblical values of welcome, compassion, and hospitality is the first step to creating awareness and strengthening a framework on which to form more active, engaged Christians who care about their neighbors individually and systemically. Our voice and values also need to impact the public square. Those who have never set foot inside a church only know about who Jesus is through his followers' words, deeds, and actions, and people will form opinions about Christ not just through our personal interactions with them but also through what we say and do in public, and what we do not say and do not do.

Speaking Up and Truth Telling as the Foundation of Advocacy

Speaking up and telling the truth about refugees as individuals made in the image of God who deserve to be treated with dignity and respect is the first way we can remind people of our common humanity. It's often easier for us to "love our neighbors as ourselves" when we believe what happened to them can happen to us. Truth telling is the foundation for advocacy because the pursuit of how our world should be must be informed by the character of God. We begin by reminding the public that everyone is made in the image of God, and we are to affirm the image of God in every person through our words and deeds.

Proverbs 31:8 exhorts us to

> Speak out for those who cannot speak,
> for the rights of all the destitute.

Proverbs exhorts us to use our voice to shape our society according to kingdom values. While we are called to be stewards of our resources and gifts, we are also called to be stewards of our influence and use our voice to speak up for the common good. When we don't speak up, it can indicate that we accept the status quo. Or, perhaps, we're concerned but we don't believe that our voice will make a difference. Speaking up allows us to push back against the darkness and to express to a society that is watching that things are not as they should be. When we use our collective voices to speak up, it can change how society operates and treats the vulnerable. When we don't use our voice, we create a vacuum in which others will speak for us.

Speaking up is crucial whenever we face injustice because current injustices will not change without a collective voice and action of the people. When it comes to refugee and immigration policy, speaking up is particularly important because so much misinformation is spread that harms the image of God in a refugee, and an "othering" happens that distances us from building relationships with the very people God has placed in our communities and calls us to love.

Speaking up can happen at various levels. It can happen on an interpersonal level, in having one-on-one conversations with friends and families about what we believe and what's happening in our communities. It can also happen within larger group conversations, when we ask questions, probe, and assert our values. We also speak up online when we share articles, write commentary, and post images of things that move us. Speaking up can also happen directly to our elected officials, to people in power who can change a situation. Such advocacy is important because it's the job of our elected officials to represent the viewpoints of their constituents, and they make important decisions every day that impact people we care about.

Saturday Night Live had a spoof about slacktivism, "Thank You, Scott," in which a man named Scott sat on a couch and shared articles and commented on articles highlighting social justice challenges that moved him. They were poking fun at the fact that individuals feel like they're changing the world by doing something as simple as changing their social media profile picture, but in reality it doesn't amount to much. It's a lazy sort of activism. And while it's true that a social media post may not change the world, social media can be a powerful tool used by individuals to raise awareness by sharing stories, sharing facts, and organizing people to a common cause. For example, the campaign led by World Relief and the National Immigration Forum informs and mobilizes evangelical Christian women through social media, primarily Facebook, to create Christlike hospitality in their communities and be advocates for immigrants. Through succinct Bible studies, powerful videos, and informative webinars, this group has become a powerful voice to serve immigrants through ministry and advocacy.

Your story and experience are the most important aspects of your advocacy. Speaking up about your values—why you believe and think the way you do, how you've changed in your thinking, and how the issues have impacted you personally—is oftentimes more important than knowing the nuances of policies or legislation. It's important in speaking up that you not attack or devalue the person with whom you disagree but assert your values, use reason and facts, and back up assertions with your own experience and story to influence others in their perspectives.

Church Advocacy

One of the strongest church advocates for refugees World Relief has worked with is Johnson Ferry Baptist Church in Marietta, Georgia. Several members of that church started volunteering with the World Relief Atlanta office in 2015, forming a "Good Neighbor" team that walked alongside several Syrian refugees who were resettled to the area. This small group of volunteers became actively engaged and started engaging their senior pastor at the time, Bryant Wright, in their ministry. Pastor Wright preached about migration from the pulpit, and he even wrote a letter to the governor to express support for refugees in the state, work that was featured in a *60 Minutes* interview focused on refugee resettlement. The advocacy the church has carried out for refugees is rooted in their friendship with refugees themselves. Churches like Johnson Ferry are not just willing to serve refugees but are also willing to use their voice and position of influence in the community to speak up for the dignity of their refugee friends and neighbors.

Other churches like Willow Creek Community Church have expansive compassionate care ministries and have also advocated for immigration reform with Congress. Their leaders have met locally with elected officials and have flown to Washington, DC, to speak at press conferences and meet with congressional leaders. As their church has served many immigrants, they've realized that to truly love and serve their immigrant neighbors holistically, they needed to use their influence as a church to have local elected officials support policies that would allow their neighbors to fully thrive.

College students have also been active on their campuses advocating for refugees. When the governor of Arkansas visited John Brown University, students held signs at chapel asking him to welcome refugees to the state. The students have been active organizing and educating the student body about the refugee crisis, even tracking and supporting legislation in Washington, DC, that would increase the US refugee admission ceiling.

Speaking Up For versus Speaking With

I accompanied Fidel Nshombo, a Congolese refugee who was resettled to Boise, Idaho, on visits to Capitol Hill in Washington, DC, as he spoke about the importance of the refugee resettlement program. He had a powerful story of being displaced when he was just twelve years old, and he is an incredible poet who has raised a lot of awareness in Boise of what's happening in the Democratic Republic of the Congo. When we met with one of the senators from his state, the senator was moved deeply by his story. More than anything I could have said on the policy side, this story will likely stick with the senator and help shape his decision-making framework when it comes to refugee policy decisions.

Advocacy can be carried out in three ways: (1) by the poor—empowerment; (2) with the poor—accompaniment/partnership; and (3) for the poor—representation.[4] Each of these is important, but the first is often the most powerful. While it's commonly thought that those marginalized do not have a voice themselves, it's important to have refugees lead the conversation and focus on their voices to guide us. They are directly impacted and thus have the strongest voice to speak about issues they understand firsthand. Their stories and experiences allow us to understand the complexities and nuances of complicated human decisions that refugees make in their journey toward freedom. Fidel is a delegate of the Refugee Congress, a collective body of refugees in the United States who organize together, advocate with their elected officials, and share their stories online. They've organized advocacy events in Washington, DC, and are some of the most powerful advocates in the country for refugees. They are the face of a successful American story. Having fled challenging circumstances, many refugees come to the United States with very little but build for themselves new lives, contributing vitally to the communities in which they live.

Advocacy Influencing US Refugee Policy

Such advocacy changes situations and systems at every level. The Refugee Congress has been instrumental in Congress's support of positive policy changes, including supporting the refugee resettlement program through robust funding. But simple acts also can be noticed by our most powerful leaders. In 2016, a six-year-old boy, Alex, from Scarsdale, New York, was so moved by the images of the Syrian civil war that he wrote a letter to President Obama, in which he asked him, "Remember the boy who was picked up by the ambulance in Syria? Can you please go get him and bring him to my home?" The president read this letter at the UN, exhorting the international community to do more to assist and protect refugees. This letter by a young child spoke to the power of advocacy—an honest, compassionate response by a young child could be used in an address by the US president in front of a global body like the UN to exhort the international community to take action. Alex later met President Obama in the Oval Office, and the president commended him on his advocacy.

That summer, 2016, World Relief launched a campaign to get people to write individualized messages to the president telling him why they would support accepting refugees to the United States. This online campaign drew messages of support from throughout the United States and the world. World Relief partnered with Oxfam and several other organizations to deliver a little over 110,000 postcards to the White House, all on a flash drive. Some of the messages were printed out on postcards and read in front of senior advisers to the president, which gave them the political support to make more bold decisions supporting refugees around the world and in the United States.

Through such advocacy efforts, the political will was created for the United States to lead the UN Summit for Refugees and Migrants in the fall of 2016, the first-ever gathering by the UN General Assembly to address refugees and migrants. This summit led to the New York Declaration, an unprecedented commitment from countries to support and protect refugees around the world. Raising awareness, writing letters, organizing public protests, media outreach, and prayer are all critical components of public witness, or speaking your values in the public square.

Public Expressions of Witness

One of the greatest benefits of living in a vibrant democracy is the ability to influence the policies and decisions of our lawmakers by raising our voice. It's often said that politicians put their fingers in the air, testing which way the political winds are blowing. It's the people's job to change the direction of the wind. In early 2017, when President Trump signed an executive order within his first month in office that banned people of certain nationalities from coming into the United States, even if they had a visa, and suspended the refugee resettlement program, hundreds of people mobilized at airports to wave signs to welcome immigrants as they first landed and to protest the ban. Lawyers huddled in airport coffee shops to strategize and offer legal assistance to individuals who were held up by Customs and Border Patrol (CBP) as they arrived.

Shortly after the executive order was signed, We Welcome Refugees, a grassroots social movement led by Ann Voskamp and Vickie Reddy to welcome refugees, organized a rally to pray for refugees outside the National Prayer Breakfast, an annual event that gathers pastors, policy makers, and foreign dignitaries to pray for the United States and the world. Around two hundred protesters held signs in the freezing cold, using their feet to walk and their voices to pray for refugees. Such an act of public witness to pray for the vulnerable outside the halls of power, to remind policy makers and religious leaders as they streamed inside to a comfortable, warm building, of simple biblical ideas like welcome and hospitality served as a stark contrast to a watching public that sometimes public prayers and actions are ways for Christians to participate in the restoration of what's broken in our society.

As such public protests were happening, we at World Relief also knew that many other evangelicals wanted and needed a place where they could support the same values of hospitality and welcome in the public square. We organized a public letter, signed by hundreds of pastors, from every state in the United States, that said, "Compassion and security can coexist, as they have for decades. For the persecuted and suffering, every day matters; every delay is a crushing blow to hope." This letter was published as a full-page ad in the *Washington Post* and was signed by some of the most prominent pastors in the country, including Tim and Kathy Keller, Stuart and Jill Briscoe, Max Lucado, Brenda Salter McNeil, and others. For these individuals to speak out like this was an act of protest. The letter created a public sense of community that emboldened the signatories to teach, preach, and serve immigrants without feeling alone. And it was a public statement that shaped a national conversation about who evangelicals were and what they stood for. These leaders offered an alternative evangelical viewpoint to the dominant narrative that evangelicals were anti-refugee and unwelcoming toward immigrants. The voices of these leaders healed the ongoing divisions that the national debate had opened and helped direct the national conversation toward biblical values of compassion, justice, and truth.

Biblical Examples of Advocates

There are many examples of advocates in the Bible—individuals who used their talents, resources, and position to challenge those in positions of authority to change a situation. Moses was an advocate whose heart broke for the people of Israel, and God chose him to speak to Pharaoh to free them from oppression. Esther spoke bravely to the king about an evil plot by one of his advisers to kill the Jewish people. And we have so much to learn from the story of Nehemiah.

Nehemiah is a classic example of a leader who used his voice, position, and resources to help defend and rebuild a system that he believed was needed to protect the people of Jerusalem. What we see in his story is that (1) his heart broke for the people of Jerusalem; (2) he prayed and fasted for God to work through him; (3) he used his voice to speak up to people in power; and (4) he gathered people around him who shared the vision with him.

Nehemiah was an ordinary person in an extraordinary position. He was not a priest or a prophet, individuals with divine appointments and spiritual authority, yet he was placed in the high political position of cupbearer to the king. As the Israelites returned home from exile, Nehemiah had his mind on the political affairs of Judah. When Nehemiah heard his brother report that the people of Judah were living in "great trouble and shame" (Neh. 1:3), he "sat down and wept" (Neh. 1:4).

Every day in the news there seems to be another story of a boat full of migrants being rescued in the Mediterranean or of a family trying to cross the United States–Mexico border. Being aware of the suffering in this world is the first step to taking action to correct it. Awareness in and of itself begins to form our hearts to understand what's happening in the world, and from that understanding, to use our talents, gifts, and resources to respond. When our hearts break to hear such stories, God can use our brokenness to fill us with his hope to love our neighbor as ourselves.

Upon hearing the news of Judah, Nehemiah didn't go to social media and post about it, nor did he go to his friends and start talking about it. He poured his heart and soul out to the Lord. It says in Nehemiah 1:4 that "When I heard these words I sat down and wept, and mourned for days, fasting and praying before the God of heaven." Nehemiah then prays a prayer of worship and confession, and requests that God grant him success and favor in order to do what he felt was weighing heavy on his, and God's, heart. When we are moved in our hearts and distressed about the circumstances around us, Nehemiah teaches us to take our heartaches and longings to the Lord first.

After praying and fasting, Nehemiah asked the king for permission to return to Jerusalem to help rebuild the wall. He was bold in his request: he also asked for letters of support that would provide him the protection and resources he needed to rebuild the wall (Neh. 2:5, 7–8), which the king granted. The king also sent army officers and cavalry with Nehemiah.

Nehemiah teaches us that we are not called to do justice alone. In fact, Scripture promises that a community of helpers, aides, counselors, friends, and others will come alongside us in the work that God has called us to do. Nehemiah had a brother who first informed him about ruinous Jerusalem, and priests and others rebuilt the wall. Nehemiah could have easily felt overwhelmed at the task in front of him, but he worked with others and their gifts to do what God had called him to do. God doesn't call us to help restore society by ourselves; he always calls us to do it in community with one another.

Nehemiah is just one example of God using people to influence political officials and the broader public to seek justice and serve the poor. In the United States, in just the past seventy years, the church has been influential in advocating for civil rights, in reducing the stigma of HIV/AIDS, in caring for and adopting orphans, and in supporting immigration reform, while also serving our neighbors through direct services. The use of our voice in the public square can help heal divisions, bring forth the truth, and ultimately create a society that more reflects values of the kingdom of God—and hence is part of the church's evangelism. Speaking up is not easy and can lead to dissension and conflict, as Nehemiah learned when he rebuilt the wall. But choosing to speak up and use our voice is choosing to fight against the status quo and injustice, which can determine whether, and fundamentally alter how, our neighbors experience true shalom and flourishing.

The Bible is full of individuals using their voices to speak up to create structures and systems to protect and provide for the vulnerable. Advocacy is a critical tool for those who follow Jesus to create a world that reflects the very values he taught in Scripture—care and concern for the marginalized and oppressed by addressing root causes of poverty and injustice. It is when we love our neighbors through our individual interactions with them, as well as by creating systems and structures in which they can flourish, that we will see glimpses of "heaven on earth," as Jesus prayed in Matthew 6:9.

Jesus Our Advocate

Nehemiah, Esther, Moses, Jeremiah, Nathan, and others in the Bible are powerful examples of advocates. But the greatest advocate of all in the Bible is Jesus himself. We advocate because Jesus is the ultimate advocate on behalf of humanity. The Bible says that Jesus is literally our "advocate" or "paraclete" in Greek. First John 2:1–2 says, "My little children, I am writing these things to you so that you may not sin. But if anyone does sin, we have an advocate with the Father, Jesus Christ the righteous; and he is the atoning sacrifice for our sins, and not for ours only but also for the sins of the whole world." It is through his death and resurrection that mankind can be restored as we are reconciled with God. Thus, being a voice with the voiceless is a reflection of the work Jesus Christ did on our behalf. We, as ambassadors of Christ (2 Cor. 5:20), must intercede on behalf of those who are suffering, in poverty, or without protection to influence those in positions of power who can save lives.

As long as injustice plagues the human condition, there will be a need to speak up and use our voices in the public square. In the Old Testament, God used prophets to speak about his kingdom values when injustices grieved his heart, but now, we as the church have that opportunity. Advocacy must become a core part of our discipleship as followers of Jesus because interceding for others is exactly what Christ did for us. The good news of Jesus is that he calls us to care holistically for others, to care about people's souls, but also to care about their physical, economic, and social condition. Advocacy can heal and create the very systems and structures that we all need to truly experience the shalom of the kingdom of God.

~~~ ONE PERSON'S STORY ~~~

My parents emigrated from India in the '80s and had a difficult time
transitioning to the United States. They decided to move, with their two
young daughters, from bustling Jersey City to a small southern town.
I was four when we arrived in a predominantly white town with no Indian grocery stores, no temples, no Indian festivities, and not another
Indian person within sight.

A few years later, there was a knock on our apartment door. Standing
there was a couple who invited me to vacation Bible school (VBS), a
weeklong camp for kids that was a lot of fun, where I would learn about
Jesus. I asked my dad if I could go, and he said yes. In hindsight, that
yes was a big deal. It's rare when a Hindu parent allows a child to attend
church. I told the couple I could go. For the next four years, they would
faithfully arrive every Sunday in a van belonging to the church's bus ministry to pick me up.

I became a part of that church, but I was still an Indian child, so I worshiped Jesus on Sundays and worshiped Hindu gods with my parents
on the weekdays following the familiar ritual of *pooja*. In church, I felt
and experienced the stirring of the Holy Spirit, the love of God and his
people. At home, I felt nothing but emptiness from the idols I worshiped
with my family. So I built a relationship with the God who was alive and
real to me and gave my life to Christ. My childlike faith had led me to a
Father who saw me and my family in our poverty and our struggles to
adapt to a small town with no family nearby.

I was encouraged to share the good news with my parents, and so
I did. I vividly remember taking them individually out to a special spot,

telling them that I did not want them to go to hell and awkwardly leading them in a salvation prayer. They were ambivalent, rather than supportive, to what they saw as my Christian phase. I was Indian, and therefore Hindu, and that was something that couldn't be changed. Just like my hair being black and my eyes being brown.

I grew up in conventional Southern Baptist churches. I remember the people who loved me well, Sunday school teachers and others who regularly demonstrated God's love and kindness to me. Though they didn't understand my background or Indian culture in general, they made sure to be supportive, understanding, and kind.

But the church was also a difficult place for me. I found my identity being slowly absorbed in southern, white church culture. I rejected my Indian heritage. I wanted to fully embrace the southern, American Christian culture where the American part got as much emphasis as the Christian part. Young and impressionable, I couldn't tell the difference between the essence of the faith they were teaching me and its American trappings.

Underlying it all was an unsaid expectation for me to assimilate.

For me to change all my beliefs, to disregard my mother's generations of traditional Indian culture, including what I ate, what I worshiped, and what I celebrated. For me to become like them so they didn't have to be uncomfortable to meet me and my family where we were.

But, in my late twenties, I began to find Christian friends at church who embraced my culture. They celebrated the things that made us different, rather than fearing them. In return, I began to shed my false identity as a Southern Baptist, basically white Indian girl, to become an Indian American girl who fell in love with a God who pursued her and changed her life in the best of ways. It took time, but God knew my sorrow and the damage that had occurred, and he brought friends into my life to help heal me. They are different ages and races, coming from different places, cultures, and denominations, but together we are the church. Their openness, gentleness, acceptance, and love have helped me begin to find my way back.

One Person's Story

Years after my dad passed, a family friend told me that my dad knew the church would take care of us if anything ever happened to him. Even if the church of my childhood was imperfect, they loved me so much that even my parents could sense it.

—*Bela Shaw*

6

EVANGELISM THAT RECONCILES

Torli H. Krua

In many ways my life and refugee journey are unusual, to say the least. My refugee journey is also typical because I believe God has been with me and that my journey is a true revelation of how God has always walked with his people from the beginning of creation. Whether we are talking about Noah, Job, or any refugee, one thing is always true:

> The LORD is near to the brokenhearted,
> and saves the crushed in spirit. (Ps. 34:18)

And, yes, God answers everyone who calls on his name, including me. "Call to me and I will answer you, and will tell you great and hidden things that you have not known" (Jer. 33:3). So, as this chapter addresses reaching out to refugees and immigrants with the good news, it is important to know that I write as a refugee myself whom God has rescued.

The purpose of this chapter is to demonstrate how Christians can leverage the truth of God's presence (light) in their engagement with refugees and other immigrants of diverse languages, races, and nationalities. This will dispel darkness, dissolve differences, transcend language and cultural barriers, and most importantly bear fruit through evangelism that reconciles foreigners and strangers who do not yet know God with God and also with ordinary American Christians, to the glory of God. Reconciliation has not only made walking with God possible; it has also brought humans from diverse races, languages, cultures, and nationalities into one family. "There is no longer Jew or Greek, there is no longer slave or free, there is no longer male and female; for all of you are one in Christ Jesus" (Gal. 3:28).

Unlike many refugees coming to America nowadays from predominantly Muslim countries who need to learn a new language, navigate new social, religious, and cultural systems, as well as deal with the trauma of war, I arrived without the usual challenges of language, culture, and lack of resources. I was not a stranger when I landed in America as a refugee in 1990. Nearly a decade earlier, in 1982, I first visited the United States upon the invitation of Massachusetts-based Wang Computers. In the 1980s, I traveled regularly to the United States as a businessman. The son of a Baptist pastor and Liberian citizen, I spoke fluent English and had a good education; a well-paying job, along with bank accounts in Boston; and an ability to travel freely between Africa, Europe, and the United States.

Given this uncommon background for a refugee, my refugee journey (which I share more of later) and current lifework serve as a significant bridge between the typical refugee and Americans with no refugee experience. My journey also lends an important insight into providence, evangelism generally, and more specifically, evangelism that reconciles. My model of evangelism within refugee communities, which I term "From There to Here and Back," views refugees through the lens of God's providence and how God orchestrates history as described in Acts 17:20–28. Because God is allowing refugees to be brought to America in the twenty-first century, I believe Westerners traveling overseas for evangelism must begin in their neighborhood. Our neighbors are refugees who hold the keys to the kingdom of God being expanded among people groups with whom other Americans would likely never have any meaningful connection.

I see the role of refugees in evangelism that reconciles in Matthew 24 when Jesus predicts unprecedented violence and destruction on a global scale due to wars and natural disasters in the last days. There Jesus also predicts the unusual spreading of the gospel worldwide before the end comes. "This good news of the kingdom will be proclaimed throughout the world, as a testimony to all the nations; and then the end will come"

(Matt. 24:14). I believe the experiences of wars and disasters ignite in refugee Christians purpose and faith that uniquely contribute to the spreading of the gospel in the last days (Matt. 24:8, 6, 14).

A strategy I commend is to leverage the presence of refugees in Western nations to ignite global evangelism that reconciles God and humans and brings reconciliation within the human family. Although less known to American churches that still send missionaries overseas, this evangelism that reconciles is reviving and reawakening both refugees and other Americans by creating new pathways for the gospel in new relationships. Working together, refugees and Americans must obey the command of Jesus: "'You shall love the Lord your God with all your heart, and with all your soul, and with all your mind.' This is the greatest and first commandment. And a second is like it: 'You shall love your neighbor as yourself.' On these two commandments hang all the law and the prophets" (Matt. 22:37–40). By working together rather than separately, US-born churches and immigrant churches can reach more people more effectively and love God and neighbor more fully.

Let me give you some background on my life and show you how this evangelism that reconciles worked in my life. I grew up in a remote village in Liberia. Born to Rev. Mahn and Esther Krua in the town of Tappita, I grew up among thirteen siblings along a dusty road that led to the village of Ziah, where my father established the Ziah Mission Christian School, a coeducational boarding school. Following in his footsteps, I founded the Ziah Faith Baptist Church. In Ziah, much as the majority of villages in Africa, there was still no electricity in 2019, no paved roads, no running water, no telephones, no television, and no one owns a car. It was in Ziah that I gave my life to Jesus at a young age and began my life's journey.

The Ziah Faith Baptist Church also served as an acclimatization post for incoming missionaries. Over the course of my youth, approximately a dozen Baptist missionaries—mostly from the United States—came to stay with my family. Together with my father and his guests, I would go on weekly soul-winning trips into the surrounding villages. Thus, from an early age, I was sensitized to the role of Christianity in reconciling people of diverse races, languages, and nationalities who had been enemies when American settlers first landed in Liberia.

Reconcile What? Evangelism That Hurt in Liberia

I also experienced evangelism that hurts. America's colonial history of slavery and racial segregation affected how Americans treated people of color in American churches and how missionaries treated people on foreign mission fields. This is best illustrated by the impact of missionaries on my upbringing. From their arrival in Liberia in 1933 until 2019, all the missionaries I ever saw in Liberia were white people. They lived in racially segregated residential communities at the Baptist mission station in beautiful homes for whites only. Even though we would sometimes go on "soul-winning trips" together, contrary to the Liberian culture of hospitality, the missionaries never welcomed black children into their homes nor ever shared meals with Africans. The contradictions were painful. They sent their children to whites-only schools and attended whites-only annual missionary conferences, which never featured a single black pastor or teacher. At Liberian church conferences, missionaries got special seats at the dinner table and taught black people. Although the missionaries received financial compensation and support, they never paid my father any money for his acclimatization services, food, or accommodation. "God will pay you," they would say.

In the eyes of their supporting American churches, foreign missionaries were heroes, but to Liberians who bore the brunt of their actions, they were often hypocrites who preached love but practiced what felt to us like hatred for blacks. But it didn't matter, because only the missionaries got the final say and got to write all the reports, with no input or comments from Liberians. The missionaries were plaintiff, judge, and jury. The views of Liberian Christians never got heard and didn't matter to the mission agency, missionaries, or sending churches because Liberians were clients, not donors contributing money.

Back to my story. After I was promoted to fifth grade, I moved twenty-five miles to Tappita to attend junior high school. In Tappita, I lived on the wrong side of the Baptist missionary station campus in the black people's quarter, called "Christian Town," which was a dilapidated, impoverished community built by missionaries for black Bible students preparing for ministry. It had no electricity (although the electricity generator supplying the missionary residence on campus was closer to Christian Town). There was no running water, no indoor plumbing. I, like most children in Christian Town, traveled about two miles to fetch water from an unsanitary open-pit water well called Jeremiah. It was common for missionaries to beat black children accused of picking mangoes or oranges that fell from trees on the massive campus. I experienced abuse and beating at the hands of a missionary who falsely accused me of stealing.

After junior high graduation, I moved another 100 miles to attend high school. After graduating from high school, I moved 150 miles to Monrovia, where the country's only university was located. At that time the Dutch government began offering scholarships to talented African students to learn about telecommunication networks. Most African countries still suffer from the crushing legacy of colonial infrastructure development, making communication between neighboring African countries more expensive than communication with European colonial nations. Liberia was an American colony in Africa.

Stories of Miracles and God Using Refugees to Reconcile

My story, like the biblical story of Hagar, is an example of ongoing miracles God works in the lives of desperate refugees throughout the ages. "And God heard the voice of the boy; and the angel of God called to Hagar from heaven, and said to her, 'What troubles you, Hagar? Do not be afraid; for God has heard the voice of the boy where he is'" (Gen. 21:17).

How did a child from a remote village get educated, find a job working with an international firm on three continents, and end up being uprooted as a refugee displaced in Boston? But God's hand can only be appreciated in the telling of more of my story.

After studying abroad and graduating from an institution in Sierra Leone in 1979, I went to work for the Liberian Telecommunications Corporation, the government-owned telephone and telegraph company. I later founded a tech company, High Tech Applications, Inc. (HTA), with dreams and aspirations of growing the company into a continental and even global technology giant.

It was a normal warm May evening in 1990, and I had gone to sleep in my apartment in suburban Monrovia, Liberia. Suddenly, at 4:00 a.m., men armed with AK-47s stormed into the apartment to take me away to be executed because of my ethnicity and association with Boston, Massachusetts, the home of Wang Computers. The insurgents, who had ties to Boston and who launched the armed invasion of Liberia, attacked the country at Nimba County, my home. The government responded by labeling Nimba people rebels and secretly killing members of my tribe. My tribe and my association with the Boston-based Wang made me a target.

Captured by brutal armed men in a war that claimed over 250,000 lives, I was staring death in the face. Terrified that I would be killed with no way of escape, I pulled my ID card and said, "Hey, I work for the government of the United States!" This was true in a roundabout way, as I worked for Wang on a contract with the US State Department, servicing computers in US embassies throughout the world. "If you kill me, you are in trouble! They will surely come after you!" I said firmly. "You liar—you don't work for the United States. You are a rebel and a rebel supporter from Boston," said one of the armed men.

Upon close inspection of the identity card, they discovered it was my photo and the seal of the US government on the back. The tide instantly turned. I was swiftly downgraded from a candidate for execution to a hostage to be released on payment of ransom. I walked away from an execution! Like many refugees, I literally "passed from death to life" (John 5:24)!

The negotiation for ransom began, and when it was finished I was free and eventually driven in a US embassy van the thirty-three miles from Monrovia to the airport, where I boarded a Sabena Airways plane to Brussels, Belgium. It was a miracle! But with war raging in Liberia, I returned to fulfill contractual duties at the US embassy in Brussels, where I was denied a visa to travel to America and later denied entry to the Gambia. I was stuck with nowhere to go. But God had a plan. It was when West African peacekeepers arrived in Monrovia that I was able to return to war-ravaged Liberia after various travels, only to find my Monrovia office of HTA broken into, ransacked, and all the computers stolen. The thief had also decided to overturn every filing cabinet in the office, but in so doing, he flipped over a filing cabinet that contained one of my expired passports, which still had a valid US visa! If only I could renew the passport, God had miraculously provided a visa for me to go to America on a special assignment of evangelism. So I flew to Sierra Leone, was able to get the passport renewed at the Liberian Embassy, and boarded a British Airways flight to Boston. I was safe. It was a miracle!

As a result of God's mercy, today I am a church planter within refugee communities. My refugee-led church plants are sending former refugees as missionaries from the United States to their war-ravaged homelands, including former Muslims. This is the "From There to Here and Back Again" approach. Most Americans are unaware that refugees don't come to America to live and die; many receive everlasting life and return to their homelands as business and civic leaders and as Christian leaders who bring the Word of God to their own people in their native languages and cultural settings.[1] How did this happen? Acts 17:20–28 is crystal clear that God is orchestrating history! He assigned human beings to their appointed families, races, and villages, and he maps out their boundaries and appointed times.

Refugees know about the brutality and ruthlessness of war. They also appreciate the value of peace. "And through him God was pleased to reconcile to himself all things, whether on earth or in heaven, by making peace through the blood of his cross" (Col. 1:20). In their search for peace, refugees from forty nations have been led to the Prince of Peace by my role as an evangelist. I equip them to be effective witnesses in America and in their native countries. Most Americans have not discerned that it is God who is sending refugees to America. Many refugees have stories of God's hand in their rescue. Hence, when American people reject refugees sent by God, they are unwittingly working against God's plans of salvation.

To illustrate this, consider the story of Kadijah, who came to America as a Muslim refugee and returned to her native country as a Christian missionary.[2] Kadijah was in the United States during the war in Sierra Leone. She was quite lonely. An elderly Christian lady befriended her and helped her to feel at home by taking her to hospital appointments, taking her shopping, and helping her navigate the complex transportation and other systems in the city. Eventually she invited her home and later to church, where Kadijah heard the gospel. She gave her life to Jesus. When asked to get baptized, she refused, citing her desire to first get the permission, approval, and blessing of her Muslim father, who lived back in her native country. Her Christian friends thought she was crazy. "It's a free country! You can do whatever you want," her friends told her.

Kadijah put the matter in prayer. Although afraid initially, she finally mustered the courage to call her father to tell him the "good news." "Father, I got a degree from a university in Boston," she said.

"Thank God!" her father exclaimed.

"Father, I met Jesus and he changed my life," she added.

"Who is Jesus?" he asked.

"I have a new faith—I am now a Christian," she said.

Her father was stunned and angry. "Why would you do such a thing to leave the true religion I taught you?" he asked.

"God revealed to me the straight Way—Jesus is the Way, the Truth and the Life."

"Did Americans deceive you to change your mind about your religion?" he asked.

"God revealed Jesus to me as the Way, the Truth and the Life."

The dad paused for a moment and reflected. In the Qur'an, Muslims pray daily, asking God to "show them the straight way to God."[3] "My daughter, if God truly showed you the way, I will not argue with God. You have my blessing, my protection and permission to go ahead and get baptized as a Christian," he said. Kadijah was overwhelmed with joy at the miracle of his reaction.

Because of her father's blessing and protection, when the war in her country was over and hostilities ceased, she decided to return to her native country, where she currently lives as a missionary among her people. When she announced she was returning to her war-ravaged homeland, her American Christian friends objected. "There is no electricity, running water, hospitals or jobs. Why are you returning home?" they asked. Worse, although for the past thirteen years as a missionary she has built a church in her village and operates a primary school for boys and girls, Kadijah is yet to see her work embraced and supported by her American church family. Refugees like Kadijah know God is transforming lives in our neighborhood and around the world, using refugees as instruments of reconciliation.

Reconciling Americans and Refugees

After Jesus's resurrection, he called his disciples to follow his example of unconditional love. With Jesus in heaven preparing a place for his followers, his task of reconciliation has been entrusted to his followers on Earth. All Christians, irrespective of nationality, social class, race, education, or profession, are tasked with evangelism that reconciles. To his disciples, Jesus gave a new commandment to love, make disciples, and bear fruit. But how can we love and make disciples in situations where people hate us or are different from us or speak languages we don't understand or are living illegally and breaking the laws of our government?

Americans are at home. Refugees are looking for a home. Americans are at peace, but refugees fleeing wars are looking for peace and peaceful coexistence. Americans enjoy freedom, including freedom of religion. Refugees yearn for freedom. Americans have privileges, benefits, and rights. Refugees in their homelands experience fewer privileges, no benefits, and no rights. Clearly, a huge chasm exists between refugees and Americans, making the task of evangelism and reconciliation seemingly impossible.

Like refugees fleeing to America today, many European Jews fearful of Hitler were searching for a safe, welcoming country for their families. Many countries refused to welcome Jews for fear of Hitler. Some desperate Jews violated the laws and illegally entered unwelcoming countries just to save their lives. Generations of Jewish refugee descendants and the children of citizens who objected to Jewish refugee immigration three-quarters of a century ago have been reconciled today as citizens of one nation. While the citizenship of these reconciled earthly countrymen is temporary, Christians must focus on the potential of refugees' eternal citizenship in the kingdom of God as reason enough to welcome refugees and thereby take the first step toward reconciliation.

The gap is further complicated by the history of colonialism. Imagine a reversal of sorts for a moment: How would modern-day Americans feel if they had been conquered or colonized by foreign powers in recent history? And then had their resources extracted by those nations? Years later, when war or persecution occurred and Americans sought asylum in the nations that had subjugated and destabilized their land, or had benefited economically, the American immigrants were treated like unwanted burdens or invaders—even though they worked and paid taxes? Can Americans imagine what this would be like? When Europeans came uninvited to America, Africa, and Asia to establish their colonies, they brought with them new languages, cultures, systems of governance, and religions. In occupying these "new worlds," Europeans enriched themselves at the expense of indigenous people they met on the land. It's reasonable to assume that many indigenous peoples and their descendants regarded European immigrants as invaders in much the same way some Europeans and Americans view new groups of immigrants and refugees as uninvited invaders. There is great need here for reconciliation.

How do we practically begin when the differences are so many and complex? I believe that with faith in God, unknown languages and the unfamiliar cultures are equal-opportunity catalysts for advancing the gospel for anyone eager to follow Jesus, because the Holy Spirit does empower us to overcome our differences. As Christians, we only need to show up, and the Lord will do the work of evangelism and reconciliation through us. A classic case of transcending differences by showing up is the story of Jonah. The huge differences that led Jonah to flee from his role disappeared when he showed up and the entire city of Nineveh was evangelized and reconciled. They wore sackcloth and poured ashes on their heads in repentance.

A common posture that exacerbates division and hinders evangelism and reconciliation is spectatorship. Most Christians across America are watching something or someone without taking part as doers. We have to show up *and do*. For example, you may watch the US Open or the NBA championships for ten thousand hours without scoring any points or gaining any skills or knowing how to play these sports. Instead of merely listening, watching others, or studying God's Word, Christians must be *doers* now. If we were to extricate spectatorship from our faith journey, the fire of revival would be ignited. Doing so involves stepping out in faith even when money is not available (Luke 10:1–6).

The Bible is replete with examples of people who were doers of the word of reconciliation and not spectators. Esau, the aggrieved party, ran to meet Jacob. Joseph, the betrayed brother, welcomed his brothers who sold him as a slave. David, the fugitive, spared the life of King Saul, who was seeking to kill him. Jesus went out of his way through Samaria and asked the Samaritan woman for water to drink. "Be doers of the word, and not merely hearers." James 1:22 calls on Christians to move beyond mere hearing, watching, and studying the Word and to avoid self-deception. While spectatorship works best at sports arenas, at cinemas, and on Broadway, bearing fruit as Christians requires faith in action: doing what God commands. Faith in action works everywhere—on college campuses, in marriages, on the job, at schools, in prison and in chains, like Paul and Silas. Note that even when the chains were broken, all the prisoners didn't run away in their case. Action faith survived in the fiery storms of Shadrach, Meshach, and Abednego. In the twenty-first century, while there are still fiery furnaces for those who will follow Jesus, he still walks in the fiery furnace with his followers.

But what do we do practically to start the journey of reconciliation and evangelism? I have observed seven helpful steps of building relationships, evangelizing and reconciling among refugees despite differences of nationalities, cultures, and languages. Simply doing what the Word of God says works. "Ask, and it will be given you; search, and you will find; knock, and the door will be opened for you" (Matt. 7:7).

First Steps to Relationship and Reconciliation

Show up. Introduce yourself and greet the refugees. Take an interest in pronouncing their names properly and request instructions on how to express greetings in their language. Attempt to speak to refugees in their heart language whenever you meet.

Go to different places where refugees and other immigrants are in charge. Just go. Show up uninvited to a refugee-led church, business, or gathering. Go to where American citizens are not in charge and don't have an agenda or a service plan. Ask how you may help. Let refugees decide how you serve them.

Speak peace as a greeting. Try to express peace and love in small, tangible ways like listening to progress reports of what's going on in their native country. They are eager to talk about their country.

Ask refugees to tell you their story. How did they get to America? Be eager to listen and learn their story. Forget about how great America is and don't ask if they really like being in America. These are human beings who love their own country and cultures but were uprooted, and God brought them to your doorstep.

Ask refugees about the loves of their lives—spouse, children,
    mother, and father. Find small gifts for their loved ones.
Visit refugees and other immigrants in their homes and experience
    their culture, listening to their stories and doing what they are
    comfortable doing as activities as you get to know each other.
Make yourself a student of their culture, language, and country and
    attend their holiday celebrations. Ask the refugee or immigrant
    to be your teacher.

There Are More Similarities Than Differences

Getting over the fear of the unknown through action may seem scary at
first. However, one way I overcome my own fear of unknown cultures is
to focus on what I have in common with folks from different countries,
tribes, nationalities, and religions. I have discovered the truth of God's
Word: "Ask, and it will be given you; search, and you will find; knock,
and the door will be opened for you" (Matt. 7:7).

To a typical American Christian, it may seem that all refugees are
Muslims or are uneducated and speak foreign languages, and therefore
there is nothing in common to focus on. However, Hebrews 11 seems
to be describing the life of refugees and their journeys of faith. Indeed,
there are a lot of similarities between all refugees and early Christians.
Read Hebrews 11.

And what more should I say? For time would fail me to tell of
Gideon, Barak, Samson, Jephthah, of David and Samuel and the
prophets—who through faith conquered kingdoms, administered
justice, obtained promises, shut the mouths of lions, quenched raging fire, escaped the edge of the sword, won strength out of weakness, became mighty in war, put foreign armies to flight. Women
received their dead by resurrection. Others were tortured, refusing
to accept release, in order to obtain a better resurrection. Others
suffered mocking and flogging, and even chains and imprisonment.

They were stoned to death, they were sawn in two, they were killed by the sword; they went about in skins of sheep and goats, destitute, persecuted, tormented. . . . (Heb. 11:32–37)

So, what are some of the similarities between Christians and refugees, then and now?

Seven Similarities between Christians and Refugees

Christians	Refugees
Christians have passed from death unto life spiritually (John 5:24).	Refugees have passed from death unto life literally.
Christians have new life, having transitioned from citizenship of their earthly country of birth to a new nationality in the heavenly kingdom of God with new laws, a new family, a new song, a new hope, and a new Master. Our citizenship is in heaven, where the Lord Jesus Christ lives. And we are eagerly waiting for him to return as our Savior (Phil. 3:20–21; 1 Pet. 1:4).	Refugees coming to America have new lives and live under new laws and new authority. By getting a green card in the first year, they take up new residency and new citizenship in their fifth year.
True Christians who follow Jesus do not invest all their resources on Earth. They are laying up their treasures in heaven, where Jesus, their loved one, resides. Store your treasures in heaven, where moths and rust cannot destroy, and thieves do not break in and steal (Matt. 6:19–21).	Refugees send remittances to where their family and loved ones reside.

Christians have found freedom because they have a relationship with Jesus, the author of eternal salvation and freedom. "So if the Son makes you free, you will be free indeed" (John 8:36; see Isa. 61:1).

There is a perception worldwide that America is the land of peace and freedom. Refugees in America have freedom, privileges, benefits, and protection.

Christians know Jesus as the Messiah, the Prince of Peace. "Peace I leave with you; my peace I give to you. I do not give to you as the world gives. Do not let your hearts be troubled, and do not let them be afraid" (John 14:27; see Isa. 9:6).

Refugees are searching for freedom and peace, which can only be found in the Prince of Peace.

Christians are waiting for Jesus's return to establish a kingdom of peace in the new heavens and new earth (Rev. 21:1–6).

Refugees are looking for a new home and are running away from their unsafe, or corrupt, or violent, or unjust native homeland.

Christians look to a future of diversity—a new diverse family of people from every tongue, tribe, and nation. Together they raise their voices in singing a new song. "After this I looked, and there was a great multitude that no one could count, from every nation, from all tribes and peoples and languages, standing before the throne and before the Lamb" (Rev. 7:9).

Although we do not want to draw much analogy between the United States and the future kingdom of God, refugees in America pledge allegiance to a new diverse country with citizens from every nation in the world. They now sing a new song, the American national anthem.

Conclusion

I am a refugee. Refugees are not monolithic. Some are Christians; some are lawyers, farmers, doctors; some are Muslims. But all are human beings made in the image of God. God loves refugees and orchestrates their survival and walks with them for his purpose. For Christians who follow Jesus's words that call us to serve refugees and other immigrants, it is easy to see that we should lay down some of the privileges and power we have to enter into mutual leadership with ethnic and immigrant leaders. This will include things like taking a genuine interest in the stories, issues, history, and struggles of refugees; respecting and deferring to refugee leadership; and loving all refugees, Christian and non-Christian. Just as darkness melts away upon impact of the weakest candlelight, seemingly huge differences between Americans and refugees dissolve and fade away when viewed through the lens of Scripture: "Be doers of the Word." Make contact with refugees. Serve refugees on their terms, not yours. Upon contact with refugees, the differences will disappear and more similarities between refugees and Christians will emerge, grow, and glow, as relationships and friends are made. The scriptural lens illuminates the person of Jesus, so that refugees see Jesus in the life and actions of their new American Christian friends. With refugee-led diaspora missions growing within refugee communities, a new evangelistic partnership with refugees will begin bearing witness to the gospel in America as well as worldwide through returning refugees. The end goal of evangelism that reconciles is a diverse humanity in harmony with God and each other, and refugees are a strategic part of this process. "*After this I looked, and there was a great multitude that no one could count, from every nation, from all tribes and peoples and languages, standing before the throne and before the Lamb . . .*"

~~~ ONE PERSON'S STORY ~~~

Nidia migrated from Mexico to Illinois shortly after the year 2000. She took the long and difficult journey with her young daughter and infant son. They fled violence and poverty, seeking to join her husband, who had migrated to Illinois three years earlier. Her hopes of starting her family life anew in the United States were soon met by despair. Her first few weeks in Illinois were the beginning of months of abuse from her husband. Without any family or friends in the area, and without knowing the language, it was difficult for her to seek help. However, when she witnessed the physical abuse of her children, she decided to leave. A neighbor helped her and her children get to the nearest bus station and to pay for tickets to North Carolina. A rural town in North Carolina, where she had family, became her new home. It was there that she found a steady job and where her children grew up.

One evening, after returning home from work, there was a knock at the door. She heard several voices speaking English outside, and feeling uneasy, decided not to open the door. She simply said: "No English!" She was surprised to hear a voice in Spanish say: "No se preocupe. ¡Yo hablo Español!" (Don't worry. I speak Spanish.) The way the words were pronounced made her realize that a native Spanish speaker was outside of her door. She opened the door and was met by a group of youth and a couple of adults. They handed her a flyer inviting her to a newly begun ESL (English as a second language) program at a local church. The program offered transportation, meals, and child care with tutoring, which made it easier for Nidia to begin participating.

The first day she participated in the program she realized that one of the persons who had come to her home to invite her was a pastor of the church. In fact, she was surprised to see the pastor participate in every session of the program, helping volunteers provide care for and tutor children, as well as set up meals. He would always welcome the students as they arrived, would sit in class with them on occasion, and would spend time with them during meals. He would engage students in conversation to hear their stories and share his own. The fact that the pastor was not constantly inviting students to attend church services, talking about the Bible, or preaching to the students attracted her attention. After a couple of months in the ESL program, the pastor invited her and her family to attend a Comunidad de Fe, or community of faith, which was a weekly gathering in the pastor's home. The gathering was simple and informal. It was centered on a common meal, to which attendees would contribute. After eating together and enjoying conversation, the pastor would invite the participants to a time of reflection on Scripture and intercessory prayer. It was in the Comunidad de Fe gatherings that Nidia began to learn about the Bible and about the relevance of prayer. It was there that she experienced God's transformative love in the context of community. It was there that she heard and came to understand the message of the gospel. It was there that she came to faith in God through Jesus Christ. Nidia is now one of the core leaders of the church she attends, where she serves in the areas of women's ministry and community outreach.

—*Rev. Edgar Vergara*

7

THE GREAT CONCERN + THE GREAT COMMANDMENT = THE GREAT COMMISSION

K. J. Hill

Missions is a big deal at the Summit Church. It's one of the main reasons I moved my family to Durham, North Carolina, and accepted a position there as the community development and outreach pastor. We believe that everyone who is a follower of Jesus has been sent by God into the world to make disciples, in much the same way that God sent Jesus into the world. Jesus prayed for this in John 17:18: "As you have sent me into the world, so I have sent them into the world." We take this so seriously that we changed the name of our missions team to the sending team. One of our four value statements is, *we send every member*. But missions, for a long time, had a very specific connotation. Missions had primarily been about going somewhere outside the United States with the primary objective of evangelism.

A Church with a Sending DNA

Missions or sending has always been in our church's DNA. Our pastor, J. D. Greear, spent a few years overseas as a missionary with the International Missions Board (IMB) of the Southern Baptist Convention. When he came back to the United States, he thought it would be temporary in order to finish his graduate degrees and maybe get married, before going back overseas. However, while he was back here in seminary, he was asked to pastor a declining church in Durham called Homestead Heights Baptist Church. He believed God was saying he could fulfill his missionary calling by pastoring a church that would send missionaries overseas. He often says there are three options for God's people—go, send, or disobey. Since it didn't seem like God was sending him overseas, he believed God was calling him to send people. So, after becoming the pastor of Homestead Heights and rebranding it the Summit Church, Pastor J. D. laid out the plan to the three hundred people that remained to be an outward-facing church that would reach the city and the world. Over the last seventeen years, Summit has sent 1,052 people overseas as full-time missionaries or to cities around the United States as part of one of our fifty-eight independent church plants. I'm not comfortable promoting numbers—I'm only saying all of this to emphasize that sending is a really big deal to our church. It's why we say things like, "We judge our success not by our seating capacity but by our sending capacity."

Surprisingly, this sending DNA was actually part of our church long before Pastor J. D. arrived. He certainly deserves credit, but maybe more as a steward or developer, because this movement we have been experiencing is part of something much bigger than us. In the 1960s, a man named Sam James was planning to move to Vietnam as a missionary with the International Mission Board. Sam was a student at Southeastern Baptist Theological School in Wake Forest, North Carolina (the same school Pastor J. D. went to), training to be a missionary. However, just before Sam and his family were to leave, doctors discovered a medical condition in one of his children that required the family to stay Stateside to get medical treatment. Sam and his wife were wondering what they would do, since their hearts had been set on moving overseas. Soon a group of people in Durham enlisted Sam in an effort to reach their neighbors. After months of outreach and meeting, this small group decided to organize a church. That church became Homestead Heights Baptist Church. Pastor James preached only one sermon at the newly formed church. He had received the call that his family was to immediately leave for Vietnam, and now that medical treatment for his child had been completed, he could respond to the call. Sam spent the rest of his life, four decades, serving overseas.

We didn't learn about the story of our founding until we were preparing to celebrate our ten-year anniversary in 2012. Some of our pastors were at the IMB headquarters in Virginia and recognized Sam James's name on one of the buildings. They began doing some research and discovered a little more about his story, and that he was still alive and well and now living in the States. We invited him to our staff retreat that year and to preach to our church at our anniversary, which was ten years for Summit but forty years for Homestead Heights. While he was with us, we learned so many incredible stories about his life and ministry, including stories about his championing racial integration in the church he pastored in the late 1950s. This was remarkable on many levels, but mainly because we had been sensing our own need to repent and take seriously God's call for unity and vision for a multiethnic church. We could clearly see Pastor James's message and demonstration of God's love for the whole world connecting directly with what we were experiencing and championing now.

It was a helpful reminder that God is the one with the mission and the vision. He is the one who moves the nations and orders the seasons. Sometimes it is tempting to think that if we just create the right methodologies, the fruit is automatic. I think that large, growing churches like Summit are especially vulnerable to this kind of thinking. We can associate numeric growth with God's endorsement and blessing. What makes it complicated is that sometimes that's true, just not always. So, we can't always associate outcomes with inputs. In John 3, Jesus is explaining to Nicodemus, one of the leading religious teachers of his day, that the Spirit, like the wind, is unpredictable. We can't contain or harness him. Yet we often reduce the Spirit and ministry to formulas, expecting to predict results by managing the right inputs. If we do this certain ministry or say these specific words, then the Holy Spirit is guaranteed to respond in the way we want. I have to remember that it's not my strategies that produce fruitfulness. It is God that makes anything fruitful. And even the term "fruitful" has to be defined according to his standard.

I had started working at Summit near the end of 2010, after unsuccessfully trying to make it as a professional soccer player and then coaching collegiately for ten years. My wife and I sensed God leading us to Durham, even though we were unsure exactly of what was ahead, having only a strong sense of wanting to align our lives with marginalized people. Summit provided an opportunity for us to learn while leading, so, in the spring of 2011, we decided to relocate with our four daughters to Durham. I still felt new to the church and community in 2012 when Sam James came to our church. I was so grateful to have a connection to this humble servant, and hearing his story and of his love for people brought lots and lots of tears. Just prior to coming to Summit, I was an associate pastor at an interdenominational church and also running a nonprofit and learning a lot about community engagement. I had participated in and even led lots of unhealthy, paternalistic community events, like toy drives and clothing pantries, with various churches, nonprofits, and government agencies. I had really good intentions, but I was ignorant and arrogant. Which seems worse than just being ignorant or just being arrogant. It's painful and embarrassing to think about.

The saddest part is that many years earlier, I had been introduced to many important concepts that should have kept me from making so many mistakes, but I didn't make the connection. While I was getting my MA in marriage and family therapy, I served as a juvenile probation officer. My degree program was a systems-based approach to therapy. I spent two and a half years studying the impact of systems on behavior and change. I spent six months seeing the futility of an agency trying to address just one part of the system and only one aspect of the person, yet expecting holistic change. When it came to church, evangelism, and ministry, I wasn't connecting the fact that we are all complex beings that are part of complex systems. Which means that people aren't simple. And interacting isn't simple.

Yet, my community engagement and missions strategies treated people like it was all simple and formulaic. I was about volunteerism with one-size-fits-all methodologies that reduce people to zeros and ones. Because of oversimplification and an overemphasis on efficiency and effectiveness, missions and engagement can often lead churches to create ministries that are more about what is convenient, and can address one aspect of a person, which is usually a material lack of some sort. This often turns into big events to draw crowds or create situations that draw attention, thinking that if we can just get people to show up, we can knock it all out quickly. People become projects. Productivity is prioritized over relationships. When we do talk about relationships, we really just mean a single, one-way conversation that is trying to force a gospel presentation or pointing out a failing or shortcoming of the people we are wanting to engage.

The problem is that this type of ministry is often conceived in isolation or with people who look and think just like we do, and we don't even realize how removed we are from the community we want to engage, so removed that we can't see how our event is offensive or insensitive or robs people of dignity. What is ridiculous is that while leading these types of ministries, I would have said it was all about loving my neighbor. I didn't even realize that I was the one defining how to love my neighbor, and my neighbor felt like a project or charity case. What was just below the surface was the self-righteous notion that I knew what was best. When Jeremiah, in 17:9, says that the heart is deceitful above all things and desperately wicked, I think he had me in mind. My heart is so deceitful that I can even make loving my neighbor primarily about me. My neighbor wasn't an autonomous person for me to get to know and discover God's gifts and glory woven into him or her—he or she was a trophy for me to display.

Learning to Love Our Neighbor

A few years before I began working with Summit, I went to a few workshops on community engagement hosted by the ministries of Dr. Tony Evans from Oak Cliff Bible Fellowship.[1] I was both convicted and inspired after discovering the way that his church was loving their neighbors. Through Dr. Evans I was introduced to Dr. John Perkins[2] and the

Christian Community Development Association.[3] I was learning so much about the importance of real authentic relationships that are cultivated by long-term, consistent presence and service and affirmation of dignity, which are all aspects of healthy community development. I was also learning so much about myself and the depths of my own sin and self-righteousness that were wrapped up in my version of Christianity. So, by the time I started working at Summit, I had a new picture of community development and church engagement.

What is remarkable is that at about this same time, Summit was rethinking their missions strategies and realizing they needed to be even more engaged locally than they had been. At the first staff meeting I attended at Summit, the staff was wrapping up a discussion about *When Helping Hurts*, by Steve Corbett and Brian Fikkert.[4] This book had challenged Summit in the ways they did ministry both locally and internationally. One of the main points of the book is that poverty is not just a lack of something material but fundamentally broken relationships with God, self, others, and the world. This means that everyone is broken, not just the materially poor. It also means that by simply addressing a material lack, one might not actually be addressing the core issue. The solution requires a commitment to getting to know other people *and* yourself. The timing was great. We were both ready and eager to change.

But change is a slow process, especially for institutions. And our institution had become large and by some measures successful, which can sometimes make change even harder. However, prioritizing real relationships and really loving our neighbors mean that we needed to do the hard, slow work of change. We were realizing the comprehensive message of the gospel, which tells us that God loves us and has done everything to save us not because we earned it or deserved it or had potential, but because of his mercy and kindness toward us. If we confessed this and really believed this, then our love for our neighbor ought to look like that kind of unconditional love.

That represented a seismic shift for us. We realized the most foundational thing that we were called to do in response to loving God was to love our neighbor, for the simple reason that everyone is made in the image of God and deserves to be treated with dignity and respect because of whose image we bear. Over the last several years, we have been trying to eliminate ministries and methodologies that don't communicate the immeasurable worth of our neighbors. I wish I could say that everything has been great and that we only engage in authentically loving ministry devoid of paternalism and selfish ambition, but of course that's not true. We still struggle to prioritize people and keep our pride in check. But we're committed to growing and changing and being sanctified.

We have learned that it is really important to answer the *why* behind loving our neighbor. How we answer that question determines our strategies for ministry as well as how we measure success. When things are challenging, it helps to remind ourselves of how central and important it is to love our neighbors. So, we decided we needed to study theologians and practitioners to help us answer the *why* question. It is hard to remember where all our ideas and strategies came from. People like Tim Keller, John Perkins, Rosaria Butterfield, Tony Evans, John Stott, and Bob Lupton have all helped us, and continue to help us, through their writings and teachings and conferences.

An Equation for Loving Neighbors

I once heard Dr. Carl Ellis talking about the Great Commission (Matt. 28:18–20), the Great Commandment (Luke 10:27), and the Great Concern (Mic. 6:8). This was helpful to me because I saw all three of these passages as foundational for understanding how to live as a Christian. I decided to start putting them together to make sure we understood how they relate to one another: Great Concern + Great Commandment = Great Commission. It's not lost on me that I have created a formula to explain how we ought to organically love our neighbor. I just want to make sure that we hold everything in balance and don't oversimplify the complexities of people and relationships. However, this formula is intended to help us see relationships among three primary things. When God's people humbly submit ourselves to his priorities and obey his command to love him and our neighbors as ourselves, then we will carry out his commission. But this also means that if we leave out any part, the equation is incomplete.

Many of us have treated the Great Commission as if it were the only thing Jesus said, and we have reduced it to a mere call for evangelism. This reductionism can lead to methodologies that prioritize isolated evangelism, often at the expense of loving our neighbors. This then becomes our metric for measuring obedience, and sometimes even maturity. We seem to forget that Jesus also said that loving our neighbor is part of the great commandment and explains all the rest of the Bible. I'll talk about this more later, but it is really important to note that I believe wholeheartedly in evangelism as the divinely appointed way for people to hear the good news of what God has done through Jesus. I just believe that evangelism is simply a part of loving our neighbor, a very important and necessary part, but still just a part. The equation doesn't work if we fail to see that evangelism is part of loving our neighbor and therefore part of the Great Commission. A comprehensive view of loving our neighbor should lead us to conclude that people are emotional, physical, and spiritual beings with systems that impact them, and loving our neighbor means caring equally about all those dimensions.

In *Christian Mission in the Modern World,* John Stott says, "It comes more natural to us to shout the gospel at people from a distance than to involve ourselves deeply in their lives, to think ourselves into their culture and their problems, and to feel with them in their pains. Yet this implication of our Lord's example is inescapable."[5] This is especially true when our neighbors are refugees and immigrants. There were times when some of our ministries were so focused on the proclamation of the gospel and sharing our faith that we didn't consider the culture, the problems, the pains of what some of the refugee families had gone through to escape religious persecution in the countries they had fled. We weren't mindful of their trauma or the context they were coming out of; we were just so intent on proclaiming the gospel that we weren't very loving. It's not that the gospel isn't relevant or even loving, it's just that the timing and methods weren't thoughtful and loving.

Jesus tells his disciples in Matthew 28 to go and make disciples of all nations, baptizing them in the name of the Father and the Son and the Holy Spirit and teaching them to obey *all* that he has commanded them. The Great Commission is Jesus sending his disciples to go do what he had been teaching them and modeling for them for three years, which included both proclamation and demonstration. When Jesus sent us as the Father had sent him, this is what he was doing—sending us to make disciples, just as he had made disciples. Jesus taught them what it meant to love God with all their heart, soul, mind, and strength, and their neighbors as themselves. Jesus wasn't just about rhetoric and stories. He modeled loving God and neighbors, and he did it by including, pursuing, and prioritizing the marginalized. He challenged the leaders who had reduced loving God to a formula that appeared right on the outside but was arrogant and self-righteous on the inside.

When he gave them the Great Commission, he wasn't giving them new information that he had forgotten to tell them about. He wasn't suddenly shifting his methodology toward only proclamation and evangelism. He told them that the way to make disciples is to teach them to obey all the commandments. Well, Jesus summarized all the commandments in Luke 10—love God with all your heart, soul, mind, and strength, and love your neighbor as yourself. Teaching people to love God and love their neighbor is central to the Great Commission. Matthew, Mark, Luke, John, Paul, and James all refer to the Great Commandment as the key to obeying all of Scripture. It would seem that if Jesus and nearly every New Testament writer is emphasizing the importance of loving God and our neighbor, that should hold the appropriate amount of weight in our teaching and discipleship. However, it's interesting that loving God, others, and ourselves isn't just instructive for knowing how to obey God; it is also how he intended for us to live from the very beginning. It is what we were made to do. Loving God and our neighbors creates right relationships and brings us back into alignment with what God intended. We are operating in our intended purpose. This is the biblical idea of shalom—peace in every relationship. So, this New Testament concept, loving God and our neighbors, that shows up all over, is actually connected with the Old Testament.

Doing Justice from a Heart of Mercy

From the very beginning God's intended design was that people would experience shalom. But in Genesis 3 we learn that sin in the form of pride brought brokenness into the world and destroyed the right relationships that we had experienced with God, ourselves, others, and the world around us. The story of the Bible is God restoring everything back to the way it was intended to be. Jesus's death and resurrection are at the apex of the story and provide both retribution for sin and hope of restoration that we can experience in part now but one day will be fully realized. The biblical narrative tells us that there can't be peace or shalom without justice. It is God's people who are to live in such a way that protects and carries out justice as a sign of his kingdom, that is marked by shalom. This is a *huge* biblical concept. Micah 6:8 says,

> And what does the LORD require of you
> but to do justice, and to love kindness,
> and to walk humbly with your God?

Typically, we've thought of this verse as commanding three things of us: to do justice, to love mercy, and to walk humbly with God. In *Generous Justice*, however, Tim Keller points out that God's expectation for his people is actually to do one thing, to walk humbly with him. The way that we walk humbly is by doing justice from a heart of mercy.[6]

It is interesting how important humility is to God. Over and over again in Scripture we are told that God opposes the proud (2 Sam. 22:28; Pss. 18:27; 31:23; 94:2; 119:21; 138:6; Prov. 3:34; 6:17; 8:13; 15:25; 29:23; Isa. 2:12; 10:12; 23:9; Jer. 13:9; 50:31; Ezek. 7:24; Dan. 4:37; Amos 6:8; Matt. 23:12; Luke 1:51; James 4:6; 1 Pet. 5:5–6). I find pride and humility to be helpful biblical categories in such a polarized world. Our heart posture seems to be really significant and key to aligning ourselves with the things that God cares about. And God seems to align himself with the vulnerable who are relegated to the margins.

Doing justice from a heart of mercy requires humility. The Hebrew word for "mercy" is *chesed,* which emphasizes *motivation* and *attitude* and describes God's unconditional grace and compassion. Throughout the Old Testament, *chesed* is used to describe God's attitude toward his people. The Hebrew word for "justice" is *mishpat,* which emphasizes *action* and is a comprehensive view of justice that is sometimes translated as "justice" or "righteousness" or "uphold the cause of," and is almost always used with the "quartet of the vulnerable"—the poor, the orphan, the widow, and the foreigner. These were the people in society that were the most vulnerable.

One way to think of justice could be as *people getting their due.* However, we usually don't see people "getting their due" as having two sides. One side is retributive, which means people receive the punishment they deserve for doing wrong. The other side is restorative, which is actually the more common usage in the Bible and means making sure people have what they need to flourish. So, one side of justice is stopping people from doing wrong, as in Leviticus 24 (eye for an eye, etc.), while the other side is ensuring that the weak and vulnerable have what they need, as in Proverbs 31:9. But justice is even bigger than giving the poor their due and even extends beyond just sticking up for them. Proverbs 14:31 and 17:5 say that not taking someone or something they say or do seriously equates to insulting God himself! Job 29 and 31 equate not caring for the poor with a lack of justice (not just being unkind) and therefore a sin. Job also says that denying justice is a sin. So, justice is not just punishing someone for something they do wrong; it is also making sure people have what they need, standing up for them, advocating for them, and taking them seriously.

In my experience, we tend to overemphasize the punishment aspect of justice, which is why we seem to think of mercy as the opposite of justice. But because justice is both retributive and restorative, mercy can be the source or motivation for doing justice. Our attitude can be gracious and compassionate as we ensure that someone has what they need. It is God's mercy toward us that sent Jesus to take our penalty for sin and satisfy God's justice, and it is again his mercy toward us that is behind his Spirit at work in us giving us peace and producing fruit, restoring us to the relationships that God intended. Keller concludes that to walk with God means to do justice, out of merciful love. This is biblical justice and central to the idea of shalom. I think it's important to note here that justice was God's idea, and for us to talk about it and care about it is simply a recovery of a central biblical idea.

When God's people live lives marked by humility with concern for justice and love for him and our neighbors, it reflects an aspect of God's character that he thinks is important and wants people to know about himself. Almost every time God introduces himself in the Old Testament, he identifies himself with the vulnerable, as in Psalm 146 and Deuteronomy 10. God seems to go out of his way to say that he is the all-powerful, great, mighty maker of everything *and* the defender of the fatherless and widow and loves the foreigner and prisoner. This seems to be the primary way that he wants to be identified. So, when God's people identify with the poor and marginalized and pursue justice and seek peace, we are reflecting his character.[7]

This was always God's plan. The connection from the Great Concern (Mic. 6:8) to the Great Commandment (Luke 10) is the same thread that runs from the beginning of the Bible to the end, from Abraham through the church.

In Genesis 12 God told Abraham that God would make him a blessing to *all* nations by bringing shalom for all nations *through* Abraham's descendants—this was not just a prediction about the Messiah, but an expectation and an identity of people who follow God. In fact, most of the times Israel was sent into captivity were because their idolatry led them away from being a blessing and toward oppressing and mistreating the poor and vulnerable.

Jesus identified with the marginalized. We see this throughout his life: where he was born, who his ancestors and parents were and where they were from, whom he chose as disciples, whom they ministered to and hung around with, how he used his power and authority—all these things point to a God that identifies with the poor and marginalized and is working to restore shalom by carrying out justice. When the writer of Hebrews tells us that Jesus is the exact representation of God, we have to conclude that these aspects of Jesus's character and identity represent God. Listen to how Jesus himself introduces his ministry in Luke 4:

> When he came to Nazareth, where he had been brought up, he went to the synagogue on the sabbath day, as was his custom. He stood up to read, and the scroll of the prophet Isaiah was given to him. He unrolled the scroll and found the place where it was written:
> "The Spirit of the Lord is upon me,
> because he has anointed me to bring good news to the poor.
> He has sent me to proclaim release to the captives,
> and recovery of sight to the blind,
> to let the oppressed go free,
> to proclaim the year of the Lord's favor." (vv. 16–19)

Right from the very beginning, Jesus was identifying himself with the prophetic passage in Isaiah 61 that spoke of God's plan to bring shalom to everyone—especially the poor and the marginalized.

Paul and Peter and James and John all continue this same thread throughout their letters to the churches. In Galatians 2 Paul has been out establishing churches, training elders, evangelizing, and defending the faith, writing letters that would become Scripture while being persecuted and tortured for it all. He then comes to Jerusalem, after fourteen years, to get the approval of the apostles. And they tell him they see the Holy Spirit at work through his ministry, and they want him to keep going; they only ask that while he is doing all the missionary, pastor, evangelist things, he remembers to uphold the cause of the poor. Which Paul says is the very thing he is eager to do. I really think this is significant. We have created this spectrum where you are either all about pastoring, evangelism, and apologetics *or* you're about social justice and care for the poor.

Paul seems to be about both, and the apostles seem to think that being about both is important.

Throughout history, the church was known for caring for the poor and marginalized, at great cost to themselves. The Roman emperor Julian was recorded in the fourth century as saying, "[The Christian cause] has been specially advanced through the loving service rendered to strangers, and through their care for the burial of the dead. It is a scandal that there is not a single Jew who is a beggar, and that the godless Galileans [i.e., Christians] care not only for their own poor but for ours as well; while those who belong to us look in vain for the help that we should render them."[8]

Many hospitals, schools, and orphanages around the world were started for the purpose of caring for the poor and marginalized. Only in the last century have Christians lost their identity as people who uphold the cause of the poor. People who are not walking humbly by doing justice from a heart of mercy are not obeying the most foundational commandments of Christianity, to love God and love our neighbors, and therefore are not fulfilling the Great Commission. Understanding this as the *why* behind serving helps us to stay committed to a lifestyle marked by serving. It also has helped us to understand *how* we should serve.

Knowing that the Great Commission is produced by the Great Commandment and the Great Concern reminds us that our service to our community ought to be marked by humility and love, and includes both proclamation and demonstration. God's plan for making disciples includes all these things. We know this because Jesus's definition of a disciple in Luke 9:23 singles out humility in the form of self-denial and suffering. The message of the hope of the gospel was intended to be proclaimed by people who lived lives characterized by humility and love, people who demonstrated the transformational power of the gospel by prioritizing others and laying down their pride.

Jesus prayed for this in John 17. He used the idea of oneness to describe the type of relationship that Christians should have with one another. This oneness can only be achieved by humility, demonstrated in doing justice from mercy. Jesus said that if we live this way, then the world will know that God is real and will believe that Jesus came. The message was tied to lifestyle, and that lifestyle was marked by humility. Their words would have weight, and the truth would come alive because the lives they lived were marked by love. Francis Schaeffer talked about this years ago in *The Mark of the Christian*. Love must be the primary identifying characteristic of God's people.[9]

We cannot love our neighbor if we do not care about justice for the poor and marginalized. We cannot love only part of a person. I have a T-shirt of Dr. John Perkins saying that love is our final fight. We can't say we love people and care only about their spiritual life, just like we can't say that we love people and never engage them spiritually. We must see people as complex, multidimensional beings. We must care about our neighbor's physical, emotional, *and* spiritual well-being, as well as the systems that impact our neighbor. It will be a comprehensive love that sees our neighbor, as John Stott says, as neither a soulless body nor a bodiless soul but rather a body and soul in community.[10]

A Ministry Marked by Justice and Love

As our church has tried to recover the identity of biblical Christians, we have tried to develop a philosophy of ministry that is rooted in justice and demonstrates this kind of love for all people. We want all our ministries to prioritize real, genuine, mutually beneficial relationships. We want to be committed to long-term development, not short-term charity. We want to ensure that our approach includes word and deed and isn't disproportionately one-sided. We believe that Jesus did both, but not always at the same time. He sometimes led with proclamation and sometimes led with demonstration, and we want to be led by the Spirit to discern what to lead with. We believe that we will know if we are humbly committed to both listening to the Spirit and really getting to know and love our neighbors. Not as a bait-and-switch-type relationship where we are saying one thing but really after something else. We want to love our neighbor not primarily to convert our neighbor, but because we have been converted and are now walking in obedience—even if our neighbor never converts or wants to hear about our faith or the hope that we have.

In one of the apartment communities where Summit people have relocated to live in relationships with resettled refugees, we have several ministries that teach ESL or prepare people for citizenship or teach people to drive. We are up front and clear that the Bible and Jesus may be mentioned, but we are also up front and clear that there is no expectation or condition of conversion or approval to participate in or benefit from the program or the relationships. In fact, in the past, when we were relationally anemic, we did similar things with very little interest in these same kinds of programs. The difference now is that the relationships preexisted the programs because we are living as neighbors and interacting around regular life rhythms and circumstances that include things to celebrate, like jobs, babies, and graduations. As well as things to mourn. Our neighbors know of our unconditional love and concern for them as demonstrated by our long-term presence and availability during good and bad times. The authenticity of love and relationships has produced trust.

In his first epistle, Peter said we should always be ready to give an account for the hope that we have. This statement implies that someone is asking a question that requires our response. It also implies that our lives are so otherworldly, because of our humility and love, that they would prompt a question in the first place. Without a presence in communities with non-Christians, these questions can't be asked; without trust from authentic love for our neighbor, these questions won't be asked.

Vic and Michelle are Summit members and have worked with World Relief for a long time. Once they invited Saul and his wife to stay with them while they were waiting for another place to open up. Saul was a Buddhist monk. Vic invited Saul to attend church with them, and he firmly rejected the offer. His rejection of their invitation didn't change Vic and Michelle's hospitality. They remained friends after they got into their own place. Just recently Saul became a Christian, but not because Vic and Michelle relentlessly shared the gospel. They were authentically hospitable and loving. There was no condition. Honestly, there wasn't even an expectation. God used their genuine friendship to communicate his love for Saul, and at the right time the gospel was proclaimed and received.

Over the years our ministries have changed from doing things for people or leading a Bible study to getting to know our neighbors. As we get to know people, we work together to address injustices or barriers or disadvantages. Often this leads to connecting people to our networks and assisting with jobs or education or housing or transportation. It has led to teaching ESL classes or helping people learn to drive or just sharing meals in each other's homes. We have helped people start new businesses or change to living-wage jobs. We work with landlords to assist people with developing a credit history so they can move out of apartments into different apartments of their choice or into their own homes. Our ministries are diverse because our neighbors are diverse, and their interests, desires, and needs are diverse. We have been learning that as we serve our neighbors, we are getting to know our neighbors.

One Arabic-speaking neighbor loves people and interacting with them and was in need of work, but she had only a ninth-grade education. We know lots of people from our church, local universities, and seminaries who are interested in learning Arabic or getting tutoring in it. Although she had never taught before, we connected her with another tutor so she could learn how to teach Arabic and develop this interest. She now has an income and a new skill that she is gifted and passionate about. She interacts regularly with Christians, the Bible, and the gospel. There is neither pressure nor expectation, just friendship.

Our neighbors have ministered to us as well and have taught us profoundly important, biblical things about culture, grace, perseverance, community, hospitality, hard work, determination, problem solving, resourcefulness, simplicity, and contentment. And as we get to know our neighbors, we are discovering real friendships, and as is true of all real friendships, we are able to talk about all the things that are meaningful and significant to us—like our faith. But also our pain and our fears and our hopes. Learning to share deeply is part of the pathway of learning to really love one another. This pathway goes in both directions and is actually wide enough to allow us to journey together. We are mutually transformed as we learn to share our own pain, fears, and hopes. Dr. King said in "Letter from a Birmingham Jail" that "We are caught in an inescapable network of mutuality, tied in a single garment of destiny. Whatever affects one directly, affects all indirectly."[11] And this is how God intended life and ministries to be.

At Summit, we think it is important to remember that the power to love our neighbors doesn't come from greater resolve or discipline. Both resolve and discipline are important, but the power that we need comes from the work of Jesus and the power of the Holy Spirit in us.

In Luke 4, when Jesus introduced himself and his ministry, he quoted Isaiah 61, but, curiously, he left out a part of the verse. Isaiah 61:1–2 says,

> The Spirit of the Lord GOD is upon me,
>   because the LORD has anointed me;
> he has sent me to bring good news to the oppressed,
>   to bind up the brokenhearted,
> to proclaim liberty to the captives,
>   and release to the prisoners;
> to proclaim the year of the LORD's favor,
>   and the day of vengeance of our God.

Jesus left out the line about the vengeance of God. Jesus was proclaiming that he was the Messiah, come to bring peace and shalom; what he didn't yet tell them was *how* he was going to bring peace and shalom. The people listening to Jesus were anticipating a messiah that was going to come to set things right and bring the vengeance of God to unleash on all God's enemies, which were *all those people out there*.

But the surprising thing was that Jesus wasn't coming to *bring* God's vengeance but to *bear* God's vengeance![12] The peace and shalom that we are all looking for is possible only because of what Jesus did by absorbing the vengeance of God into himself. We actually can't bring justice, and in fact, we ourselves stand as perpetrators of injustice. On our own, in our pursuit of justice, we are imbalanced and inconsistent and emphasize either restorative or retributive sides of justice. We can become conceited and self-righteous, or harsh and unloving. We have wronged God and stand condemned and unable to pay the penalty, but Jesus came and took our place. Paul tells us he satisfied God's wrath and God's just punishment by dying for us. Because Jesus took our place, when God looks at us, he sees the righteousness of Christ. Jesus is the one who makes us just and the one who seeks justice. In fact, justice itself is an empty concept apart from God's definition of morality. This is the gospel message that we believe and proclaim. This proclamation is necessary to making disciples, which is what Jesus sent us to do. To carry out the Great Commission and obey the Great Commandment and Great Concern, we have to love our neighbors holistically, which means we must care about them spiritually. As we have been learning what healthy community development looks like in practice, we are also learning what gospel proclamation and gospel demonstration look like in tandem.

I'm grateful for the path that we have been on. This journey of learning to walk humbly has been full of joy and sadness, hope and pain. We're learning to love one another and know one another. It is a slow process, but God—and our neighbors—are gracious.

~~~ ONE PERSON'S STORY ~~~

While driving to my office one afternoon, I saw a woman carrying groceries down the street. Despite the 94-degree weather, she wore a long dress and *hijab*. Her arms and legs were covered, but I sensed that she felt exposed. This was a woman who not only stood out from everyone else in our predominantly white city but was also viewed as a threat because of her Muslim faith.

My heart broke as I thought about how lonely and scared I would have been if I were walking in this woman's shoes. My heart was filled with compassion for her. We had never spoken before, but I felt prompted by the Spirit to lead our missional community to pray for God to open a door that would lead us to her.

Within thirty minutes of the conclusion of our prayer meeting, we were contacted by Karen Spencer of World Relief. Karen and I had never spoken before, and she told me about an Ethiopian woman who had just moved to Paragould, Arkansas. She asked if our church would be interested in supporting this lady as she settled into our city. It just so happened that the woman she spoke of was the same woman I saw walking down the street. God heard and answered our prayers!

Within two weeks of my original phone call with Karen, we were sitting with Haji and her boys in our church conference room. Two years later, Haji moved to Louisville, but not before introducing us to thirty-one immigrants/refugees that have been in our homes and around our tables. We have celebrated birthdays, played, and cried together. We have assisted our Muslim friends with employment, citizenship, furnishing their homes, and more.

We have been told by these families, on more than one occasion, that we have loved them in ways that even their own families have not. Haji still refers to her sons as our sons. Tamrat and Hafiza often remind us that we are the only true family they have. Jibril stops by periodically to ask for dating or career advice. Ismael, upon celebrating his son's birthday with our missional community, wept in my truck as he talked about an "unexplainable type of love" they receive from us. Naturally, this has opened the door for gospel conversations with our Muslim friends, as we explain to them how the love they are experiencing is the love God has extended to us through Christ.

—*Jared Pickney*

8

EVANGELISM THAT HEALS

Samira Izadi Page

In her late fifties, she was still beautiful. She carried herself gracefully, and her mannerisms reflected a traditional Middle Eastern upbringing. As she started sharing her story with me, I sensed something strange about her, a quietus, a sort of hopelessness and dark resignation. She had been a part of the royal family in Afghanistan when the country was seized by the Soviet Union in the '70s. The Russians killed all the male members of her family, including her father, brothers, and brother-in-law, and raped her, her mom, and her sister. The three women escaped and eventually became refugees in the United States. Her mom and sister, who had lost their husbands, never remarried, and she, who had been raped at a very young age and witnessed the murder of her family, never married. As she was telling the story, her words were void of any emotion. The passage that kept coming to my mind was Isaiah 42:3:

> A bruised reed he will not break,
>> and a dimly burning wick he will not quench;
>> he will faithfully bring forth justice.

That woman was the bruised reed that never met the Messiah, never received justice and healing. Her life burned dimly in hopelessness, trapped in that tragic childhood moment because, as she shared with me, no one ever shared the healing love of Christ with her even though she had lived in the United States for over twenty years. What a shame!

Her story stood in stark contrast with my own story. I was born and raised in Iran as a Muslim. My Christian journey started at the age of six when I had a vision of the Virgin Mary. God planted a seed of love in my heart and continued to grow the seed in the form of a deep love for the church, but as a young Muslim girl, growing up in an Islamic, theocratic country, I knew little about the church and even less about Jesus. I married when I was very young to a Sunni Muslim who was eventually persecuted as part of the persecution of religious minorities in Iran. We left Iran empty-handed twenty-two years ago, with no resources or documents. God miraculously brought us to Mexico and, eventually, to the United States.

The Church as Gateway of God's Grace

On the day we arrived, in Dallas, Texas, God connected us to a Baptist church through the ministry of an unlikely person. My vision of the Virgin Mary and love for the church, along with the love I experienced from the Baptist church, brought me to the decision of conversion and baptism. The ministry of that church to a Middle Eastern family that looked nothing like them was absolutely incredible. With the help and support of the church, we started building a new life in faith. With the support of the pastor, I was admitted to seminary even though I had no transcripts or record of my prior education. Next, God moved me to the Episcopal Church, but my Baptist church remained my loving family. I was ordained a priest, and toward the end of my time as a curate, I started praying for the next stage of ministry. I started a church mobilization ministry called Gateway of Grace, which has become one of the largest refugee ministries in Texas, with over ninety partner churches and organizations in many denominations. It continues to grow.

As I prayed for a name to start the ministry, I pondered what my Baptist church had done for us and how its ministry had changed my life. What became obvious was the flow of grace toward us from the church. I was reminded that the main difference between Christianity and other religions is God's grace made manifest in the world through God's people. The church as an instrument of God in the world is the gateway of God's grace. I chose the name Gateway of Grace because it reflected the nature of Christian ministry as practiced by my Baptist church toward my family and me.

At Gateway of Grace, we emphasize that we belong to the human family. What hurts people across the world pains us. From the same dust we are all created, and from the same breath we all are given the breath of life. Christ's death was for everyone in the human family, and God's desire for all is healing, restoration, and eternal life.

We celebrate the courage and resilience of our refugee families, who are striving, even toiling, to make a new home in a new land. Try to comprehend what it is like to leave behind, with a few hours' notice, everything you have, to journey at someone else's direction, to eat only when someone feels compassion for you, all the while not knowing if there is a future and a hope. We pray for the 70.8 million displaced people who are forced to abandon their homes because of war, persecution, famine, and evil governments. For some, there was no time to sell their homes or cars or businesses. For most, this was not a problem because all their possessions had already been destroyed or taken. Regardless, they took only what they could carry on their backs. The value of their college degrees and their respected reputations have been reduced to memories that often feel like a dream. We remember those who are imprisoned, persecuted, and relegated to unsafe refugee camps, who languish in lands where there is no hope of escape. We grieve for persecuted Christians and other persecuted religious minorities, political prisoners, abused women, and victims of human trafficking. Their physical scars often pale in comparison to the severe trauma that will be with them for the rest of their days.

We acknowledge that we too were at one time spiritual refugees, roaming through life apart from God and controlled by governance of the evil one. Yet, in God's amazing grace, God poured out his mercies on us, rescuing us from the wastelands of life, bringing us into his family, giving us a home, a future, and a hope. In filling us with the Spirit, God simultaneously called us into serving, to strive for justice and peace for the least, the lost, and those hoping for a new life.

At Gateway of Grace, we are intentional about discerning opportunities to be a part of God's kingdom work in bringing hope, peace, and dignity to the marginalized of the world.

I cannot imagine what turns the course of my life would have taken without that church. Perhaps my life would be wasted in hopelessness, like the life of that Afghan woman. Perhaps God would use another church to reach out to us, but the point is the faithfulness of that Baptist church. The point is the power of church, the Christian community, the body of Christ, to transform lives. I am forever grateful to God! Writing this essay is deeply personal for me. I see the tribulations, losses, and pains that my family and I experienced, and the witness of my Baptist church as God's teaching tools and preparation for the ministry of church mobilization. God gave me a heart of deep and unconditional love for the church since my childhood, and a heart of compassion for refugees because I was one.

How Jesus Did Evangelism

When we talk about evangelism, what issues come up? We regularly talk about methodology to win people over, being more effective in getting the message across, using the media format, Bible distribution, the Jesus Film, etc. It is not often that we stop and think about how Jesus did evangelism. Or, if we do, we think that was the ancient world, and we now have new tools and methodologies, tracts, videos, and ways that are better than his ways.

Do you ever wonder why Jesus did things the way he did? Why he came into the world; lived as one of us; walked, ate, and hung out with the sinners? Healing seems to be at the heart of what he did and at the heart of his good news. According to Isaiah, the Messiah's wounds heal us. We see this in the ministry of Jesus. Looking at the Gospel of Matthew alone, for example, we see examples of healing of one individual or many in chapters 8, 9, 12, 14, 15, 19, and 21.

Some may argue that healings were signs to prove a more significant point, that he was the Messiah, the Son of God. That definitely is a part of it, but not all of it. The more significant point is that where there is the presence of God, healing naturally takes place. In other words, healing is the effect of God's presence. Just as God's essence is love, God's presence brings healing. Yes, the hope is that people can see that effect and know the person of Christ, but what if they don't? Does that change the effect of God's presence? The answer to this question is found in Revelation 22:

> Then the angel showed me the river of the water of life, bright as crystal, flowing from the throne of God and of the Lamb through the middle of the street of the city. On either side of the river is the tree of life with its twelve kinds of fruit, producing its fruit each month; and the leaves of the tree are for the healing of the nations. Nothing accursed will be found there any more. But the throne of God and of the Lamb will be in it, and his servants will worship him; they will see his face, and his name will be on their foreheads. And there will be no more night; they need no light of lamp or sun, for the Lord God will be their light, and they will reign forever and ever. (vv. 1–5)

One lesson from this powerful passage, along with chapter 21, is that the complete indwelling of God in the new heaven and the new earth brings healing for the nations. So, part of the salvation that will be revealed to us, as we read in Romans 5:9–10, Romans 13:11, Ephesians 1:14, and 1 Thessalonians 5:8, is the provision for "healing of the nations."

That is the picture after the completion of the kingdom of God. Now, however, we live in between times. We are the signs of the coming kingdom; we are instruments of God and representatives of Christ in the world. It is, therefore, only natural that we too are about the business of healing and restoration in the lives of those the Lord brings to us.

One of the striking aspects of the life of Jesus is the amount of time he spent with people, talking to them, dining with them, and visiting them. He was, after all, the Son of God. He could move a finger and do great miracles that would reveal his identity to all. He really did not need to hang out with the sinners, the broken, the sick, and the stranger, but he did. Why? One reason is that he was God. He knew what people needed in order to be healed and experience the kingdom of God.

Before I dig deeper into the Scripture, I would like to talk about the population this book is focused on: refugees, asylum seekers, and other types of immigrants. There is a legal difference between an asylum seeker and a refugee. A refugee is someone who has crossed an international border and cannot return to the home country due to fear of harm, persecution, or death. Refugees who enter the United States are processed by the United Nations. They have also been background-checked and admitted by the US government. When they enter the country, they enter legally. An asylum seeker is a refugee who has not been processed by the United Nations and enters the country and then applies to obtain legal status. Depending on their region of the world, refugee and other immigrant families arrive in America having experienced myriad difficulties, including war trauma, illegal imprisonment, malnutrition, physical assault, extreme fear, political and religious persecution, torture, abandonment, and loss of all their earthly possessions. The emotional and psychological wounds are deep and varied.

I know this firsthand. We crossed the Rio Grande to enter the United States and apply for asylum. It was one of the scariest things I have ever done. It happened about twenty-two years ago. We rose early that morning and set out to cross the border to apply for asylum in the United States. In desperation, we found two Mexican men who said they could get us across the border. They told us that we could carry only a backpack and water. When we arrived at the river, I was nearly paralyzed by fear of the high and swift-moving water. I don't swim, and just looking at the river made me dizzy. But turning back was not an option. One of the Mexican men carried my younger son on his shoulder and was moving through the river very quickly. My then-husband had my older son while at the same time trying to hold on to me. The dizziness increased, and I became even more unstable. As the man carrying my younger son got farther and farther away, my parental fears turned into panic. I was terrified that we would get separated from him or, worse, lose him to the river. I started screaming at my husband to just let me go and catch up with the man carrying my younger son. As a parent, I was willing to drown so that my sons could make it safely across.

When we finally made it across the river, our guides left us in the middle of the desert. They told us that we were in the United States. We walked for hours and hours. We were exhausted, starving, and running out of water. Eventually, we saw in the distance the bridge into the United States and a few buildings. We walked into the immigration post, told the officials our story, and asked for asylum. They were convinced we were Mexicans and wanted to send us back. As I listened to that rejection, I was filled with fear. My mouth was dry and my heart was pounding. I did something I had never done before—I begged. I did not beg for myself but as a mother. The only thing that truly mattered, as I faced the border officers, was the well-being of my children. A part of me recognized that a once middle-class, college-educated Iranian woman was now a dirty, dusty mother who was only concerned about getting her children to safety.

The experience of becoming a refugee or asylum seeker strips you of your pride and dignity. It reduces you to survival instincts, and often to feeling that you are nothing. There are wounds so deep that even today I choose not to discuss them. But God is merciful! In his indescribable way, God uses those wounds for kingdom purposes—if we will allow him. Common belief is that life's wounds heal. But that is not always true. And some wounds are better left unhealed, lest we forget and harden our hearts to the suffering of others. Lest we forget that we are mere humans and that, in the blink of an eye, our lives can turn upside down and be in need of mercy, as mine did.

In addition to the wounds and suffering, after arriving in the United States, I had to learn to survive in a competitive and capitalistic society that is overwhelming and a frequent source of stress, anxiety, and depression. The pressures can lead to marital discord and the challenges of parenting in a vastly different culture. For the most part, refugee and immigrant families do not have the support system of extended families or a church community. Lack of the English language further isolates the family, especially the mother, since she often had little opportunity for education while in her country of origin. Thousands of refugee and immigrant families strive daily to survive, and many fail, in various ways.

WWJD? (What would Jesus do?) How do you think Jesus would share the gospel with them? With a tract or Jesus Film? Would he ask them if they know where they are going after they die? As a side note, in my ministry, Gateway of Grace, I cannot count the number of times Muslim refugees have brought me a Jesus Film that a Christian had given them. They say things like, "This is about Jesus. I am a Muslim," or "You are a Christian, and I thought this was for you," or "We are not supposed to see the face of a prophet." Let's think about this for a moment. What if Jesus, instead of being Jesus and doing all the things he did for and with the people, would give the people he encountered a film of what he did? Would that make more difference in their lives than having Jesus with them in person?

To be instruments of healing in the lives of refugees and immigrants by the power of the Spirit, it is helpful to have an even deeper understanding of the wounds of refugees. I will share a few examples. Refugee families experience losses that cannot be immediately discerned, particularly by those who do not share the same experiences. Refugees and immigrants themselves may not have the ability or knowledge to explore them. This kind of loss is called "ambiguous loss." It is hard to understand and identify. Ambiguous loss usually does not have closure.

In my ministry, we serve refugees from sixteen countries. Many come from cultures and religious backgrounds where human dignity is tied to social status, wealth, marital status, number of male children, job, education, etc. In other words, human dignity is earned and can be lost. I remember an occasion when my team and I took some used but nice furniture to the apartment of a newly arrived refugee family from Iraq. The husband had worked for American soldiers as a translator. The wife did not speak English. She seemed extremely uncomfortable, but she was quick to offer us tea, cookies, and fruit. As I sat down to visit with her, she asked her husband to translate. She started telling me about her life in Iraq, her large home, her maid, and her jewelry. I immediately noticed what she was trying to do. She was trying to tell me that she once had dignity. She could not name her discomfort as ambiguous loss, but what she was feeling was the loss of dignity because of the loss of her material possessions. I cannot count the number of times my husband and I have sat down in the apartments of refugees who started showing us pictures of what their life was like in their own country.

Ambiguous loss can take different shapes and forms. As a Muslim-background believer and minister, I cannot go back to Iran. I have not seen my family in twenty-two years. My sister and brothers got married and have children, I lost my grandfather, my nieces and nephews grew up—and I missed it all. While I am aware of the kind of loss, there is no closure for it. Each time something happens in my family, each time someone gets married, has surgery, has a child, and I am not there, the wound starts throbbing. The nature of emotional and spiritual wounds of trauma is such that they cannot be seen except by the pain they cause. To bring the gospel into these painful situations, it is necessary for us to know the people we serve, share life with them, and enter into their pain.

Motivational Interviewing

The title of this chapter is "Evangelism That Heals." Let's look at a scientific methodology of emotional and spiritual healing and how it lines up with the way Jesus approached people. There are several methods for emotional and psychological healing, but I will discuss only one. Matthew Bennett is a researcher and blogger who specializes in trauma-informed care. In his book *Connecting Paradigms*, he talks about "motivational interviewing,"[1] an innovative, neurobiologically based approach to emotional healing. The question is how someone who has experienced so much trauma and pain can change and turn his or her life around. Motivational interviewing equips counselors with effective ways of communication and a set of strategies to help people bring about change in their lives. "Motivational Interviewing is a collaborative goal orientated style of communication with particular attention to the language of change. It is designed to strengthen personal motivation for and commitment to a specific goal by listening and exploring the person's reasons for change within an atmosphere of acceptance and compassion."[2] As I discussed earlier, refugees and immigrants experience trauma, and this method is relevant to them.

Motivational interviewing has four dimensions that work together:

Engage: building relationship between counselor and client

Focus: creating a shared agenda

Evoke: bringing about the expertise and gifts with which the client has the capacity to make change in his or her life

Plan: finding the right path for the desired change, and solutions and ways to achieve it

The ministry of Jesus, the great physician, reflects these dimensions and so much more. Jesus engaged people by building relationship with them, as witnessed by his feasting with sinners. Refugees and immigrants come from cultures that are shame based, and they do not readily reveal their needs or wounds. Only through deep trust and real friendship will refugees open their heart and soul to others. Many refugees never experience friendship with Americans. It is very difficult for them to open up even to other refugees about their suffering, wounds, and hurts. They do not want the shame of the revelation of their personal stories. Building relationship with Americans can be intimidating for refugees and immigrants, and in many cases, due to the material loss and the perceived loss of dignity, it can be retraumatizing. Relationships need to be built slowly in order to build trust. We have to be mindful that refugees, in particular, often have been betrayed by their own government, police force, and countrymen. Along the journey, they might have experienced abuse, cheating, and violence.

Many refugees' trials are due to religion. Building trust, therefore, is an essential part of engaging them, and it takes time before we bring the name of Jesus up with them. If we are too hasty to bring up conversations about Jesus and do things that can be perceived as a bait and switch, we risk losing relationship and retraumatizing the refugee or immigrant. In fact, forcing people into religious conversations before they are ready can hinder people's ability to receive, and it puts them on the defensive and in survival mode due to the harm done to them and their families in the name of religion. They are resettled in apartment complexes that house only other refugees. The Gateway of Grace cofounder comes from a Bible church background and is an evangelical, so his first instinct used to be sharing the gospel as soon as possible. After learning about refugees, their lives and their plight, and after relating to them, he now does evangelism in a deeper way.

I recently attended a meeting about evangelizing Muslims, where one of the speakers talked about the Jesus Film Project.[3] The meeting consisted of ministers of missions from several churches as well as other ministry leaders in Dallas. The speaker advocated going door-to-door at apartment complexes and handing out the Jesus Film to Muslim immigrants with whom no prior relationship had been established. Handing out materials while ignoring the relational and healing aspects of evangelism is both inefficient and misguided. We have to remember that refugees and immigrants are people, not our evangelism projects. We must examine our hearts to make sure we reach refugees out of an abundance of Christ's love. When my younger son was a teenager, he asked me if we could convert to Buddhism. I asked him why we should do that. He said, "Because Buddhists are good people." I said, "So are Christians." He said, "Not really. They are interested in other people only if they think they can convert them." What a sad thing for a teenager to notice, and a horrible witness.

Two aspects of motivational interviewing are "focus" and "evoke." They help us create a shared agenda with the people we are trying to help, to help them think and draw out their God-given gifts to create change. We see Jesus doing this in the story of the woman at the well in John 4. Jesus sees a woman at the well drawing water, and he asks for water. The Son of God asks a Samaritan woman for water and creates a common ground. Jesus humbled himself, and it was so surprising to the woman that she initiated what came to be a long conversation. In each sentence, Jesus helps the woman think, and at one point she draws her own conclusions about Jesus: "I see that you are a prophet." By engaging her in conversation, Jesus helps her express what she already knows about the Messiah. Jesus then tells her that he is the Messiah, and the woman becomes the first evangelist. On a cautionary note, Jesus wanted a genuine relationship with the woman. Everything else came after Jesus treated the woman as a person. Jesus did not start with an agenda but with real relationship. Jesus helps the deeply wounded woman at the well heal or overcome the consequences of her wounds.

We see the same type of relational ministry with Peter. In Matthew 16, after having done many signs, particularly the feeding of the four thousand, and after a discussion about the Pharisees and Sadducees, Jesus asks his disciples, "Who do people say that the Son of Man is?" Here Jesus helps them think and does not directly refer to himself. After the disciples answer, he asks, "Who do you say that I am?" For Peter, even in his effort to profess who Jesus is, the path is not simple. He denies Jesus three times before the crucifixion.

The last aspect of motivational interviewing is "plan." As Christians, we believe that

> The human mind may devise many plans,
> but it is the purpose of the LORD that will be
> established. (Prov. 19:21)

Evangelism is about being witnesses to all that Jesus has done, according to Acts 1:8. The rest is the work of the Holy Spirit, so we don't need to be anxious about whether we can convert a refugee or an immigrant. No one can confess that Jesus is Lord except by the power of the Holy Spirit (1 Cor. 12:3).

Refugees and immigrants, those who don't know Christ yet and have not received the grace of God through Jesus Christ, are not the only ones who need healing as it pertains to evangelism. We too need healing in our hearts and minds. In other words, evangelism is a process of mutual healing accomplished by the Holy Spirit.

Connecting with Muslims

Sometimes we may know the methods and the significance of relationships, but it is simply hard for us to connect with certain populations, such as Muslims. I frequently speak at churches and conferences. One disconcerting issue is the motivation to evangelize Muslims for many Christians—the fear of Islam, of its spread, and of its subscribers. I have seen the fear-based-evangelism approach used by some evangelists, who begin their talks by sharing how quickly Islam is growing or how the number of mosques is increasing in their community. They suggest that the need to stymie the growth of the Islamic faith is greater than the need to share Christ's good news with Muslims.

Christians, across denominations, share with me their concerns about the lack of integration of Muslims into the American culture. In response, I discuss an issue that is very difficult for them to hear. I challenge them to look at the culture of the United States and consider how appealing it is to a conservative family from the Middle East or Africa, whether Christian, Muslim, or Hindu. I ask them to consider a day at the mall or a day of channel surfing on TV. How would they, as Americans, assess those environments? What would a conservative refugee family see? Would they feel comfortable seeing some of the things that are on TV or at the mall? I ask them to consider the rate of teenage pregnancies, premarital sex, pornography, and marital infidelity. How appealing are those for a family from the Middle East or Africa to adopt automatically? Of course, not all people from the eastern and southern parts of the world are conservative. Many of them become Westernized very quickly. I have observed that men readily take advantage of the newly found freedoms in the United States, while it takes longer for women to adapt and change.

A great number of refugees and immigrants in the United States are Muslims, and the main obstacle to ministering to them is "Islamophobia."[4] Peter Skerry, a professor of political science at Boston College, compares the experience of Muslims in America as a minority group to the experience of Catholics in the 1920s. Current dominant anti-Islamic sentiments are much like the antipapal sentiments of the early twentieth century. Muslims are portrayed as intruders and are associated with various vices. Andrea Elliott, a reporter on Islam in America for the *New York Times*, told the *Harvard Political Review*, "In the aftermath of 9/11, Islam and terrorism became almost synonymous in the media."[5]

Our effort to evangelize Muslim refugees and immigrants must start by examining our hearts and praying for our attitudes. We must enter this process with an attitude of humility, not with self-righteousness and moral superiority. We must have a genuine concern for the mission of God, not for justifying our own political position about immigrants, refugees, or any other matter. We must acknowledge that we are learners and that we need each other, rather than assume that we are dispensers of wisdom and the sole fount of knowledge and God's truth. We must acknowledge that none of us is fully complete in knowing and seeing God's truth. We all are in the process of growing more into the fullness of Christ's image through loving and serving.[6] Therefore, there can be no comprehensive truth without our willingness to embrace and serve others in the name of Christ.[7] Jesus reminds us that as we do to the least of these, we do unto him. As we serve Muslim refugees and immigrants and see the image of God in them, as any other human being, we receive healing. Refugees and immigrants can discern between genuine love and the pretense of love.

In my experience, many in the church refuse to be involved in ministry to Muslims out of fear, hatred, or political conservatism. At the same time, many Muslims—particularly recent immigrants—are also afraid of Americans. They fear being stereotyped, discriminated against, associated with terrorism, ostracized, or attacked. In both populations— on either side of the asymmetrical relationship—fear and hatred result from intellectual immaturity, a lack of emotional awareness and empathy, and spiritual woundedness. Intellectual immaturity is distinct from plain ignorance. We are intellectually immature when limited, biased, or otherwise partial knowledge and (mis)information shape our perceptions. It is rooted in learning through a certain politically or socially affected lens without empathetically considering other lenses. Once a Westerner applies this perception to Muslim immigrants or refugees around him or her, a lack of empathy or emotional intelligence follows soon thereafter. Preconceived notions of Islam and Muslim culture foment into fear and hatred, creating deep spiritual wounds. It is true that the attacks of September 11 were horrific; many experienced a great loss of loved ones. But it is also absolutely true that the devil has used and will use these wounds to hinder the work of God. He will fan the flame of hatred and fear of Muslims through intellectual, emotional, and spiritual immaturity.

After September 11, we have seen American attacks on Muslims: the burning of the Qur'an; attacks on mosques, such as the threat to a mosque in Houston in June 2019; and other antagonistic acts.[8] Those attacks have not been of God, because violence is not of God. Jesus fights violence with love. As one scholar describes, "The Devil's trick is to make us let go of the good to fight the evil, and even worse, to lead us to let go of an evil we can do something about to work for an abstract and idealized good that can never be realized."[9] With devastating wars on two fronts in the Islamic world and a surplus of refugees traveling to the United States, we need a serious and practical educational process for evangelizing and overcoming the obstacles and fears that hinder God's mission.

You may wonder what this practical process should look like, and how people can begin to live out healing evangelism in this context. In this last section I will lay out six things I believe help respond to this question. Throughout the Gospels, evangelism has to do with actions and conversations. Conversations are an essential part of our humanity and relational nature. They happen naturally within hospitable environments. For the purposes of uniting the body of Christ, and for the sake of God's mission of sharing the good news with immigrants and refugees, conversations are not about problem solving. Conversations are not about lecturing others on whether what they believe is right or wrong, and they are not debates about Islam versus Christianity. Restorative conversations are about learning about each other's fears, yearnings, hopes, dreams, and prayers. Conversations are testimonies of God's work within us, among us, and through us, even when people don't know Christ and do not use those words. Real, simple, deep, and meaningful conversations even with unbelievers are the easiest way to bring about change.[10] Through this type of conversation, we realize that we belong together. We share our experiences as we share our lives. Real conversations are respectful and truthful, not shaming or judgmental. They address specific issues without being accusatory.

We now take up the six components of meaningful conversations.

Questions

A great way to start a conversation is by asking questions. Asking questions exhibits our willingness to learn. Our curiosity about the other person shows that we care. I believe that our conversations, even with our enemies, need to start on a personal note: How are you? How are things? How is your family? People struggle with different issues in their daily lives. We get to practice this kind of caring within the body of Christ and then take that into the world. If we do not care about the concerns of our brothers and sisters in Christ who might be refugees and immigrants, how can we care about refugees and immigrants who are not? If we do not care about the concerns of our brothers and sisters in Christ, then it is hard to imagine that our cares and concerns for Muslim refugees and immigrants would be genuine or rooted in God's love. We must examine our hearts to make sure that we love people out of the overflow of God's love—those who share the same values as we do, as well as those who do not. Conversations that reflect care for the person, rather than care for a cause or political view, create warmth, friendship, and a sense of belonging together.

The initial questions should be about topics that we agree on. With Christian refugees and immigrants, they can be about issues such as our common love for Christ, the church. With non-Christians, they can be about family, friendship, humanity, and peace. Finding common ground that we mutually care about helps build rapport so that we can transition smoothly into matters upon which we may not agree. In addition to hearing people's thoughts, we need to discover their feelings. We must allow them to be expressed, as harsh as they might be. What makes asking questions a successful way of moving us forward is the act of listening to the answers.

Listening

Listening can bring healing into our mind and heart so that we can share the gospel in its fullness and glory with immigrants and refugees. The Bible commands us to be quick to listen (James 1:19). Listening is a crucial element of conflict resolution. "All of peace-building can be summed up in listening."[11] We, along with those who disagree with us or come from another culture or religion, often feel unheard. Listening to one another, rather than talking past each other, helps to alleviate feelings of being ignored or unheard. Being ignored and feeling unheard can be obstacles to the mission of God. Listening to the stories of immigrants and refugees allows us to see God's work in their lives, despite what we perceive to be wrong about them or their religion. It also allows us to understand their cares and concerns and where they are coming from.

Listening helps us discover what we share in common and see the complexities of another person's experience, and hopefully helps us participate in collective wisdom. By listening, we soon discover that while facts and realities form a portion of the conversation, much of what people share, their responses that reflect fears, prejudices, hatred, and anger, are purely emotional barriers. Emotional barriers often go beyond the object of the emotions. For example, if one has a negative experience with a Japanese or a Muslim person, one can form an opinion about all Japanese or Muslim people. This means that, on the topic of refugees, the strong feelings and emotions of a few individuals can change the direction of the mission for an entire church (1 Cor. 5:6–8). Under-standing the emotional nature of the responses helps us recognize that a holistic approach, not simply an intellectual one, is needed to alleviate emotional barriers.

Contributing

After listening to others, we can contribute to the conversation by add-ing perspectives and thoughts. This is the point where emotions might be heightened. Using this method in churches can become tricky. It is best for our contribution to not be a counter to the perspectives of the other person. One way of de-escalating potential tensions is to use the word "and" instead of "but."[12] For example, I use this sentence, "We are concerned about our national security *and* the lives of the refugees who are hunted down by ISIS," rather than saying, "We are concerned about our national security, but we are also concerned about the lives of the refugees who are hunted down by ISIS." The word "but" creates a di-chotomy, which at times might be real, but in cases of Christian ministry and reaching refugees, immigrants, etc., it is a false dichotomy. Reaching refugees and being wise and safe are not mutually exclusive.

Biblical Perspective

Bringing a biblical perspective to the issue of refugees and immigrants is a very significant part of the model. In working with churches, I have come to realize that many Christians are not familiar with the biblical passages on caring for the poor, the stranger, the oppressed, the widows, and the orphans. Unfortunately, many Christians are not familiar with the ultimate plans and purposes of God for the nations as described in Scripture, nor do they know the depth and significance of God's care for the groups mentioned above. For some, caring for the poor and the stranger becomes a humanitarian cause apart from the concern for their relationship with God. For others, Christianity is a self-serving path with insurance benefits. Many Christians are concerned only with the salvation of souls as an otherworldly reality that takes place after we die.

The necessity and mandate throughout Scripture to care for physical, as well as emotional and spiritual, needs of these groups provide a great framework for fulfilling God's mission. Without this comprehensive framework, applying bits and pieces of the Bible to this or that matter can be damaging. We must be faithful to the entire Bible about the redemption of individuals, tribes, nations, and the entire creation. It is equally important to discuss both the practical and spiritual consequences of a lack of faithfulness. People usually cannot dispute what the Bible clearly says throughout the Old and New Testaments. After I share what the Scripture teaches on these issues, many come to me and acknowledge that they had no idea. For many, these teachings are truly eye opening.

Offering a biblical worldview helps alleviate both hatred and prejudice toward immigrants and refugees. It helps Christians see that, as citizens of the kingdom of God, their nationality is tied to the fate of the entire world.

Raising Awareness

Another aspect of meaningful and healing conversations has to do with facts. I cannot tell you the number of times someone has approached me at a church and said they did not know the facts. Offering facts and raising awareness are related, but they are not the same. Knowing the facts about crime in Dallas does not necessarily mean that I am aware of my surroundings. Raising awareness adds another layer to the facts that instigates response and personal involvement. Raising awareness starts by revealing realities and facts. Many Americans are only partially aware of other nations and cultures, world politics, and the impact US foreign policy has on other nations. They usually are not familiar with the plight of refugees or the patterns of migration, unless they are reported in the media. They have little knowledge of the contribution of peoples from other cultures to the US economy, culture, and scientific community. I know from personal experience that many Americans believe that all Muslims are backward, just as they believe that all Buddhists are peaceable. The opportunity to broaden the horizons of Christians to learn the facts and realities on these matters is simply amazing. Raising awareness helps mitigate hatred, prejudice, and generalizations and bring about healing.

Prayer

Prayer is the most essential element in bringing healing both into our own lives and into the lives of refugees and immigrants. It is only through prayer and the fellowship of the Holy Spirit within the body of Christ, individually and corporately, that transformation and effective evangelism are possible. Prayer is a "process of remodeling in which the believer's life is on the one hand purified from false ways of feeling, thinking, and acting which are contrary to the will of God, and on the other hand regains the likeness of the divine love."[13] It is clear that prayer is the key to the outworking of the good news of Jesus Christ in the life of the church and its outpouring into the lives of refugees and immigrants.

If we believe that the Holy Spirit leads us, we must spend time with God to find guidance and come under the leadership of the Holy Spirit. As we do that, our prayers are transformed into missional statements. We can look at our prayers, the things we pray for, matters that upset us or move our hearts, issues that burden our hearts. Then we can look and see whether they include the expansive biblical concerns for individuals and matters, far and near, or whether they are small and insular. Under the leadership of the Holy Spirit, our prayers are big and include our enemies, other nations, and people with whom we may not have anything in common. Our prayers find the shape of God's heart, who so loved the world that he gave his only Son (John 3:16).

Conclusion

When I was growing up, my mother was my best friend and like an older sister to me. Like anyone else, she has struggled with different issues in her life, some more difficult than others. As a cultural Muslim, she would never attend mosque, fast, or say her daily prayers, and for the most part, she had no apparent need for them. The past fifteen years, however, have proved to be trying years for her in ways that no human intervention could resolve. My younger brother had to be placed in permanent rehabilitation. The suffering and struggle of my brother have been extremely painful to my mother. And, like the majority of people living in Iran, my family was pushed to the edges of poverty due to the sanctions against that country.

Several years ago, I sent a Bible to my mother through two Baptist missionaries who traveled to Iran. She started reading the Bible, and God started working in her heart. In her first visit to the United States a few years ago, she went to church with me and we had conversations about Christianity. After her return to Iran, God continued to work in her heart. Additionally, God healed her from an incurable disease after her prayers to Jesus. Earlier this year, God revealed to her that she would be traveling back to the United States. That seemed nearly impossible to her, since it required resources that were beyond her means. Later in the year, God opened an unexpected door of opportunity, and she was able to come.

While she was here, I shared the gospel with her, and she immediately received it because the seeds had been planted and watered for a long time. She asked what she needed to do, and I told her she needed to be baptized. She knew that God had provided this opportunity for her to travel for the purpose of being baptized.

My mother is back in Iran now, longing for a church community. She cannot attend a registered church, and unfortunately, attending a house church in Iran can be very dangerous.[14] She describes her experience prior to her conversion as that of a blind person who had no idea colors existed, and after her conversion, her eyes were opened and she could see colors and marvelous beauty that she could not see before. Her circumstances in Iran have not changed, but God has changed how she looks at the same circumstances. My mother now has the peace of God and the strength of the Holy Spirit to live a life of hope in a very difficult place.

I share this story to emphasize the freedom and responsibility of the church in the United States. It is uniquely equipped to reach non-Christian immigrants and refugees with the love of Christ and an attitude of servanthood and humility. Heeding the warnings and advice in this book will help the church do so in healthy ways. The good news of Jesus Christ will transform practical, emotional, and spiritual darkness and hopelessness among refugees as Christians intentionally become salt and light, come alongside ethnic leaders, and learn how together to be the body of Christ for the sake of mission. My mother could pay the ultimate price for attending church in Iran. In the United States, however, those who do not know Christ and those who believe can freely experience and express the joy of being a part of a Christian community.

Equally important is reaching Christian immigrants and, particularly, refugees who have been persecuted because of their faith. It is the church's responsibility to help restore and encourage them even as they are witnesses of faithfulness to the Christians in America. Millions of immigrants and refugees need the kind of healing and hope that my mother experienced. Eternal life begins here and now. The foundation of the church rests on these truths.

Ultimately, evangelism is the mission of God and God's church. It is a privilege to take part in that mission by loving, serving, and sharing our lives with immigrants and refugees and mutually experiencing God's healing. Evangelism is about planting seeds and watering them, and sometimes we see the fruit but many times we don't see the growth (1 Cor. 3:7). Our task is being faithful to the planting and watering, and it is God who brings the growth and the fruit.

CONTRIBUTORS

Rev. Laurie Beshore served, for almost thirty years, as the founding pastor of Outreach Ministries at Mariners Church in Irvine, California. Its mission is to mobilize world changers who are courageously shaping culture while meeting real needs. Laurie lives in Southern California and has been married for many years to Kenton Beshore, her childhood sweetheart and senior pastor of Mariners Church for decades, until 2019. She is also the author of *Love without Walls: Learning to Be a Church in the World for the World.*

Rev. Andrew F. Bush and his wife, Karen, have served internationally, for almost thirty-five years, in the Philippines, the Palestinian Territories, and Israel. Presently, he is the director of the Bethlehem Institute for Peace and Justice in Bethlehem in the Palestinian Territories, as well as pastor of the East Jerusalem International Church. Previously, he was the chair of the Department of Global Service and Mission at Eastern University in St. David's, Pennsylvania. His books include *Learning from the Least: Reflections on a Journey in Mission with Palestinian Christians* and *Millennials and the Mission of God: A Prophetic Dialogue.* He holds post-graduate degrees from the École Biblique et Archéologique Française in Jerusalem and Princeton Theological Seminary.

Rev. Eugene Cho's many passions involve engaging leadership, justice, the whole gospel, and the pursuit of God's kingdom on this earth. He currently serves as the president/CEO of Bread for the World. He travels throughout the world to encourage churches, nonprofits, pastors, leaders, missionaries, and justice workers. He is also the founder and former senior pastor of Quest Church—an urban, multicultural, and multigenerational church in Seattle, Washington. He is also the founder and visionary of One Day's Wages (ODW)—a grassroots movement of people, stories, and actions to alleviate extreme global poverty. The vision of ODW is to create a collaborative movement that promotes awareness, invites simple giving (one day's wages), and supports sustainable relief through partnerships, especially with smaller organizations in developing regions. Since its launch in October 2009, ODW has raised nearly $9 million for projects to empower those living in extreme global poverty. ODW has been featured in the *New York Times*, the *Seattle Times*, NPR, *Christianity Today*, and numerous other media outlets. For his entrepreneurial work and spirit, Eugene was recently honored as one of 50 Everyday American Heroes and listed in the Frederick Douglass 200—that is, two hundred people around the world who best embody the spirit and work of Frederick Douglass, one of the most influential figures in history. Eugene was also the recipient of the 2017 Distinguished Alumni Award from Princeton Theological Seminary. Eugene is the author of two books: *Thou Shalt Not Be a Jerk: A Christian's Guide to Engaging Politics* (2020) and *Overrated: Are We More in Love with the Idea of Changing the World Than Actually Changing the World?* (2014). Eugene and Minhee have been married for nearly twenty-five years and have three children.

K. J. Hill is the Pastor for Community Development and Outreach at the Summit Church in Durham, North Carolina, and cofounder and board chairman of the ReCity Network. He has an MA in religious studies with a concentration in marriage and family therapy from the University of Mobile in Mobile, Alabama, as well as a BA in psychology from Houghton College in New York. K. J. has been a semiprofessional soccer player, a collegiate soccer coach, a teacher, a counselor, a mentor, and a pastor. He has been married to Liz, who is a Durham Public Schools teacher, for over twenty-five years, and together they have four daughters: Ana, Mary, Phoebe, and Kate.

Torli H. Krua came to the United States as a refugee after the 1989 civil war in Liberia that forced a million people to flee their homeland. Choosing to leave a successful career in business, Torli serves today as an activist and missionary to refugee communities in Boston and beyond through Universal Human Rights International, an organization he founded to promote peace and democracy in Africa and refugee rights in the United States. At Emmanuel Gospel Center, he codirects the Greater Boston Refugee Ministry. Rev. Krua is the pastor of Ziah Mission Church in Boston's Dorchester neighborhood. Torli and his wife, Saawile, have one son.

Sandra Maria van Opstal, a second-generation Latina, pastors at Grace and Peace Community on the west side of Chicago. She is a preacher, liturgist, and activist reimagining the intersection of worship and justice. In her fifteen years with InterVarsity Christian Fellowship, Sandra mobilized thousands of college students for God's mission of reconciliation and justice in the world. Sandra served as Urbana Missions Conference Worship Director, Chicago Urban Program Director, a member of the Latino National Leadership Team (LaFe), and Northwestern University Team Leader (for multiethnic fellowship). Sandra's influence has also reached many others through her leadership and preaching on topics such as worship and formation, justice, racial identity and reconciliation, and global mission. She has been featured at Wheaton College, North Park University, the Justice Conference, Evangelical Covenant conferences, Willow Creek Association conferences, and various churches. Sandra serves as a board member for Evangelicals for Justice and the Christian Community Development Association. In addition to her ministry experience, Sandra holds a master of divinity from Trinity Evangelical Divinity School in Illinois and has been published in multiple journals. She has authored *God's Graffiti Devotional*, *Still Evangelical*, *The Mission of Worship*, and *The Next Worship*.

Rev. Dr. Samira Izadi Page is the founder and executive director of Gateway of Grace, a ministry that mobilizes the church, across denominations, to serve refugee and immigrant families in holistic ways. Gateway of Grace supports newly arrived families by furnishing apartments, food and rental assistance, job search, English as a Second Language classes, self-advocacy classes, and more. Gateway trains volunteers and churches to come alongside refugee and immigrant families and support them in effective ways, the point where friendships form and integration begins. Raised a Muslim in Iran, Samira found her way to the United States after a long and challenging journey as an asylum seeker. Arriving in Texas, she was shown unique kindness and generosity by a local church that soon became a second family. Today, her experiences help her not only to serve people displaced by war, famine, political turmoil, and natural calamities but also to raise up churches and individuals to form genuine relationships with refugees despite their background, culture, or religious affiliation. Her story has inspired and challenged many—not just through her ministry but also through her sermons, speeches, workshops, TEDx talks, and various interviews, including with *Christianity Today*. Her book *Who Is My Neighbor* is used by churches to inspire and mobilize congregations. Samira has dedicated her life to bringing the hope, love, and healing of Christ to those whose hope and dignity have been stolen by oppressive governments and circumstances.

Dr. Issam Smeir is a licensed clinical professional counselor who specializes in trauma treatment for refugees, victims of torture, and severely abused and neglected children. He holds a master's degree in clinical psychology from Wheaton College, a doctorate in counseling and clinical supervision from Northern Illinois University, and a postdoctoral training certificate in global trauma with refugees from Harvard University. He is an expert in the Narrative Exposure Therapy (NET) approach. Issam, a former national clinical consultant for World Relief, currently is the founder and executive director of Shifaa for All, a non-profit organization that works with persecuted Christians around the world. Issam is a coauthor of *Seeking Refuge: On the Shores of the Global Refugee* Crisis (2017).

Ann Voskamp is the wife of a farmer, mama to seven, and the author of four *New York Times* best sellers, *The Broken Way*, *The Greatest Gift*,

Unwrapping the Greatest Gift, and the sixty-week best seller *One Thousand Gifts: A Dare to Live Fully Right Where You Are,* which has sold more than one million copies and has been translated into more than twenty languages. Named by *Christianity Today* as one of fifty women most shaping culture and the church today, Ann knows unspoken brokenness and big country skies and an intimacy with God that touches wounded places. Millions do life with her at her daily photographic online journal, one of the top ten most widely read Christian sites. Having traveled to numerous places around the world to see the plight with her own eyes, Ann has committed her life to advocate for the most vulnerable around the world. She is also the cofounder of We Welcome Refugees and had the opportunity to share this vision through her talk entitled "Hospitality to Refugees."

Jenny Yang provides oversight for all advocacy initiatives and policy positions at World Relief. She has worked in the resettlement section of World Relief as the Senior Case Manager and East Asia Program Officer, where she focused on advocacy for refugees in the East Asia region and managed the entire refugee caseload for World Relief. Prior to World Relief, she worked at one of the largest political fund-raising firms in Maryland, managing fund-raising and campaigning for local politicians. She is coauthor of *Welcoming the Stranger: Justice, Compassion, and Truth in the Immigration Debate,* serves as Chair of the Refugee Council USA (RCUSA) Africa Work Group, and was named one of the "50 Women to Watch" by *Christianity Today.*

NOTES

INTRODUCTION

1. Unless otherwise indicated, Scripture quotations come from the New Revised Standard Version.

2. Dianne Solis, "Pew: Refugee Arrivals in U.S. Decline Sharply as World Crisis Grows," *Dallas Morning News*, May 25, 2017, https://www.dallasnews.com/news/immigration/2017/05/25/pew-refugee-arrivals-in-u-s-decline-sharply-as-world-crisis-grows/.

3. Hans Urs von Balthasar, *A Theology of History*, Communio Books (San Francisco: Ignatius, 1994), 123.

CHAPTER ONE

1. The antecedents of the term *euangelion*, or good news, can be found in Isa. 52:7, which refers to the good news of God's reign. See Jeannine Brown, "The Theological Background of Euangelion," The National Association of Evangelicals, accessed April 13, 2019, https://www.nae.net/theology-behind-euangelion/. *Euangelion* is used eighty times in the New Testament. The related Greek word *euangelizo*, to announce good news, is found in various forms fifty-four times.

2. Stephen Neill, *A History of Christian Missions* (London: Penguin Books, 1966), 37.

3. Neill, *History of Christian Missions*, 39.

4. Neill, *History of Christian Missions*, 39.

5. Elaine A. Heath, *Naked Faith: The Mystical Theology of Phoebe Palmer* (London: Lutterworth, 2010), passim.

6. Michael G. Long, ed., *The Legacy of Billy Graham: Critical Reflections on America's Greatest Evangelist* (Louisville: Westminster John Knox, 2008), 3.

7. Billy Graham, *The Evangelist and a Torn World: Selected Messages from Amsterdam '83* (Minneapolis: World Wide Publications, 1983), 29.

8. See "About EE," Evangelism Explosion International, accessed May 29, 2020, https://evangelismexplosion.org/about-us/.

9. Philip Jenkins, *The Next Christendom: The Coming of Global Christianity* (New York: Oxford University Press, 2002), 2.

10. Samuel Escobar, *The New World Mission: The Gospel from Everywhere to Everywhere* (Downers Grove, IL: InterVarsity, 2003), 26. Christian mission, even in recent years, has also indirectly partnered with militarism to further its goals. See Andrew F. Bush, "Bullets and Bibles: The Unhealthy Marriage of Missions and Militarism," *PRISM* (Palmer Seminary), Fall 2010.

11. This theme is developed further in Andrew F. Bush's *Learning from the Least: Reflections on a Journey in Mission with Palestinian Christians* (Eugene, OR: Cascade, 2013), 16–40. A critical turning point for Christianity was the conversion of the emperor Constantine in the fourth century and the subsequent merging of empire and Christian faith.

12. Graham, *The Evangelist and a Torn World*, 30–31.

13. Walter Rauschenbusch, *A Theology for the Social Gospel* (New York: Macmillan, 1917), passim.

14. The subsequent congresses and study groups constitute the Lausanne Movement. The international gatherings are often referred to as Lausanne Congresses. See Lausanne Movement, accessed May 30, 2020, https://www.lausanne.org/.

15. The Lausanne Covenant, article 4, includes references to the following texts: 1 Cor. 15:3, 4; Acts 2:32–39; John 20:21; 1 Cor. 1:23; 2 Cor. 4:5; 5:11, 20; Luke 14:25–33; Mark 8:34; Acts 2:40, 47; and Mark 10:43–45. See Lausanne Covenant, accessed May 30, 2020, https://www.lausanne.org/content/covenant/lausanne-covenant.

16. The Lausanne Covenant, article 5.

17. The Lausanne Covenant, article 6.

18. J. Matthews, "Christ and Kenosis: A Model for Mission," *Journal of Applied Missiology* 2, no. 1 (1991): 4.

CHAPTER TWO

1. United Nations High Commissioner for Refugees, *UNHCR Resettlement Handbook* (Geneva, 2002), 236.

2. E. Tulving, "Episodic Memory and Common Sense: How Far Apart?" *Philosophical Transactions of the Royal Society of London Series B: Biological Science* 356 (2001): 1505–15.

3. Robert J. Sternberg, "Triangulating Love," in *The Altruism Reader: Selections from Writings on Love, Religion, and Science,* ed. T. J. Oord (West Conshohocken, PA: Templeton Foundation, 2007), 332.

4. Sherry A. Falsetti, Patricia A. Resick, and Joanne L. Davis, "Changes in Religious Beliefs Following Trauma," *Journal of Traumatic Stress* 16 (2003): 391–98.

5. R. C. Kessler et al., "Posttraumatic Stress Disorder in the National Comorbidity Survey," *Archives of General Psychiatry* 52 (1995): 1048–60.

6. D. F. Walker et al., "Changes in Personal Religion/Spirituality during and after Childhood Abuse: A Review and Synthesis," *Psychological Trauma: Theory, Research, Practice, and Policy* 1, no. 2 (2009): 130–45.

7. Anthony Fryling, "The Relationship between Posttraumatic Stress Disorder Symptoms and Adolescent Spirituality" (PhD diss., Wheaton College, 2012).

CHAPTER FOUR

1. Karen González, CCDA 2019 Conference workshop, "Beyond Welcoming the Stranger: Decentering Whiteness in Immigration Ministries."

2. Karen González, *The God Who Sees: Immigrants, the Bible, and the Journey to Belong* (Harrisonburg, VA: Herald, 2019), 75.

CHAPTER FIVE

1. Ashley Fantz and Ben Brumfield, "More Than Half the Nation's Governors Say Syrian Refugees Not Welcome," CNN, November 19, 2015, https://www.cnn.com/2015/11/16/world/paris-attacks-syrian-refugees-backlash/index.html.

2. LifeWay Research, "Evangelical Views on Immigration," February 2015, http://lifewayresearch.com/wp-content/uploads/2015/03/Evangelical-Views-on-Immigration-Report.pdf.

3. Bob Smietana, "Churches Twice as Likely to Fear Refugees Than to Help Them," LifeWay Research, February 29, 2016, https://lifewayresearch.com/2016/02/29/churches-twice-as-likely-to-fear-refugees-than-to-help-them/.

4. Micah Network, "The Church and Advocacy: Seeking Justice for the Poor," accessed June 2, 2020, https://www.micahnetwork.org/sites/default/files/doc/library/plenary_5_the_church_and_advocacy.pdf.

CHAPTER SIX

1. Heidi Shin, "A Young Liberian Refugee, Educated in America, Chooses to Move Back 'Home,'" World, July 12, 2016, https://www.pri.org/stories/2016-07-12/liberian-american-renounced-his-us-citizenship-and-then-headed-home.

2. "Torli Krua Interviews Kadijatu Wellington," YouTube, May 1, 2016, https://youtu.be/2RSIhXANycw.

3. Qur'an 1:6; for translations, see http://corpus.quran.com/translation.jsp?chapter=1&verse=6.

CHAPTER SEVEN

1. Tony Evans, "Adopt-a-School Initiative," accessed June 2, 2020, www.churchadoptaschool.org.

2. John Perkins, With Justice for All: A Strategy for Community Development, rev. ed. (Grand Rapids: Baker Books, 2007).

3. Christian Community Development Association (website), www.ccda .org.

4. Steve Corbett and Brian Fikkert, *When Helping Hurts: How to Alleviate Poverty without Hurting the Poor . . . and Yourself* (Chicago: Moody Press, 2009).

5. John Stott and Christopher J. H. Wright, *Christian Mission in the Modern World* (Downers Grove, IL: IVP, 2015), 25.

6. Timothy Keller, *Generous Justice: How God's Grace Makes Us Just* (New York: Penguin Books, 2010).

7. Timothy Keller, "What Does the Lord Require of Us? A Biblical Theology of Justice" (plenary lecture given at Formed for Justice Conference, Redeemer Church, New York City, 2018).

8. John Piper, *A Godward Life: Seeing the Supremacy of God in All of Life* (Colorado Springs: Multnomah, 1997), 253.

9. Francis A. Schaeffer, *The Mark of the Christian* (Downers Grove, IL: IVP, 1970).

10. Stott and Wright, *Christian Mission in the Modern World*, 29.

11. Martin Luther King Jr., "Letter from a Birmingham Jail 1963," in *A Testament of Hope* (New York: HarperCollins, 1986), 290.

12. Keller, "What Does the Lord Require of Us?"

CHAPTER EIGHT

1. Matthew S. Bennett, *Connecting Paradigms: A Trauma-Informed and Neurobiological Framework for Motivational Interviewing Implementation* (n.p.: Matthew S. Bennett, 2017), audiobook.

2. Bennett, *Connecting Paradigms.*

3. "The JESUS Film Project distributes the film 'JESUS,' a two-hour docudrama about the life of Christ based on the Gospel of Luke." "About the Jesus Film Project," The Jesus Film Project, February 17, 2014, http://www.jesusfilm.org/aboutus.

4. "The term 'Islamophobia' was first introduced as a concept in a 1991 Runnymede Trust Report and defined as 'unfounded hostility towards Muslims, and therefore fear or dislike of all or most Muslims.' The term was coined in the context of Muslims in the UK in particular and Europe in

general, and formulated based on the more common 'xenophobia' framework." "Islamophobia Research & Documentation Project," Center for Race and Gender, accessed June 3, 2020, http://crg.berkeley.edu/content/islamo phobia/defining-islamophobia.

5. Neil Patel, "Do Americans Fear Muslims?," *Harvard Political Review*, November 4, 2010, http://harvardpolitics.com/united-states/do-americans -ear-muslims/.

6. Susan Scott, *Fierce Conversations* (New York: Simon & Schuster Audio, 2002), 1, audible.

7. Miroslav Volf, *Exclusion and Embrace: A Theological Exploration of Identity, Otherness, and Reconciliation* (Nashville: Abingdon, 1996), 258.

8. Zain Shauk, "Masked Men Try to Burn Houston Mosque; HFD Investigates," *Houston Chronicle*, May 15, 2011, https://www.chron.com/life /houston-belief/article/Masked-men-try-to-burn-Houston-mosque-HFD -1682665.php.

9. Ann Belford Ulanov, *The Wisdom of the Psyche*, Contemporary Christian Insights (Einsiedeln, Switzerland: Daimon Verlag, 2000), 35.

10. Margaret J. Wheatley, *Turning to One Another: Simple Conversations to Restore Hope to the Future* (Gildan Media, 2008), 1, audible.

11. JustPeace Center for Mediation and Conflict Transformation, *Engage Conflict Well: A Guide to Prepare Yourself and Engage Others in Conflict Transformation* (Washington, DC: JustPeace, 2011), 3.

12. Scott, *Fierce Conversations*, 1, audible.

13. Vincent Brümmer, *What Are We Doing When We Pray? On Prayer and the Nature of Faith* (Aldershot, UK: Routledge, 2008), 96.

14. Mainline denominational churches in Iran are registered with the Iranian government. They are not allowed to share the gospel with Muslims. They are also required to report the names of all who attend the church. If a Muslim or a Muslim-background believer attends, he or she will be arrested.

INDEX